THE BUZZARD WORE A TUTU

Chronicles of Life and Adventures in New Orleans

By Errol Laborde

Illustrations By Arthur Nead

THE URBAN PRESS

© *Copyright 1994*

THE URBAN PRESS
218 South Scott Street
New Orleans, LA 70119

ISBN 0-9643874-09

TABLE OF CONTENTS

Previous Books by Errol Laborde:

Mardi Gras, a Celebration, By Mitchel Osborne and Errol Laborde, 1981, Picayune Press

I Never Danced with An Eggplant (On a Streetcar Before), 1988, The Urban Press

FOREWORD

by Sheila Bosworth

ERROL LABORDE IS A SEER.

The above warning should be printed on the cover of this book, for the benefit of those innocents who assume they can read this collection of Mr. Laborde's columns for *New Orleans Magazine* and get off lightly, with nothing more than the usual soreness resulting from excessive use of the laugh muscles. The laugh muscles get quite a workout, all right, but accompanying those twinges is residual heartache, the kind that comes of reading pure truth applied to prose by a poet's strong and gentle hand.

The *New Webster's Dictionary of the English Language* defines "seer" as "one with deep spiritual insight; a person gifted with second sight." In his new book, Mr. Laborde sets his sights on his hometown, New Orleans, writing about the place with sharp perception and wit and a lover's passion. The combination never lets his readers down. He lends us his vision, allowing us to see things the way he sees them, and it's not always a pretty sight.

"White suits keep no secrets," he reminds us, and then takes us to an uptown social event to show us how he knows. There he stands, in just such a merciless suit, immobilized and hungry, surrounded by daredevils who are not intimidated by their own snowy suits, darting about, tossing down dripping oyster patties. Many of the things Errol sees worry him, and seeing them through his eyes, we begin to worry, too. "Carnival is so delicate," he writes, "there is so much that could go wrong on the streets, that I always felt some relief when the last Comus float rolled by." Reading that, you start to fret about what might befall Mardi Gras should Errol ever quit keeping an eye on it.

Errol looks upon the things he loves with passion, ordinary things such as snowball machines, with their "endearing purpose of changing ice into snow," All Saints' Day picnics beside a pond at a cemetery, a bar where the band plays songs by The Drifters in Cajun French and City Park in summer at dusk, a place where he sees evidence that "God is a tennis player."

He sees danger all over the Gondola at the World's Fair and on the Zephyr at Pontchartrain Beach and makes us laugh at it, but in a firecrackers combination of "glitter, celebration and instant gratification" he sees something of the character of New Orleans itself, and so he loves the illicit little devils. Looking backward and forward simultaneously, he sees reason to rejoice in the city's present and future as well as to mourn its past: "There are those who lament that the Quarter is not what it used to be," he tells us. "To that I answer that it never has been what it used to be . . . today's experience is tomorrow's nostalgia."

Mark Twain wrote that "the secret source of humor itself is not joy but sorrow." The writing in Errol Laborde's latest collection taps that secret source brilliantly, but let certain prospective readers beware: read this book while you're far away from New Orleans and you risk that residual heartache mentioned earlier. The author of this book, after all, is homesick for New Orleans even as he lives each day here, and he's extremely good at sharing the feeling with his readers. The places he takes us to — such as an old soda-fountain drugstore serving its last lunch to customers, or a jazz wake on North Claiborne Avenue — break your heart while they make you hungry for a bowl of gumbo at noon and the sound of a bass playing in the night. He makes us feel "sadness because of the departed, and joy from the music," no easy feat for a writer or even for a magician.

"The Buzzard Wore A Tutu" is a treasure of a book. If Errol Laborde didn't exist, then New Orleans in her wisdom would surely have invented him.

Sheila Bosworth is the author of the novels "Almost Innocent" and "Slow Poison," of which *The Washington Post Book World* reported: "'Almost Innocent' was a very tough act; 'Slow Poison' proves to be not merely a worthy successor but one that expands Bosworth's territory in breadth and depth."

Commenting on "Slow Poison," *The Cleveland Plain Dealer* observed: "enchanting . . . It is here in the territory of the human heart, seen through the disorienting smoke of New Orleans, that Sheila Bosworth is a true and exciting guide." *The Los Angeles Times* noted that, "New Orleans has to be the most exotic city in America, and Bosworth writes about it as well as, if not better than, anyone else."

INTRODUCTION

Chapters in books are usually clearly marked and are announced in a Table of Contents. In everyday life, however, the beginning of a new chapter is often less conspicuous. Over lunch at Antoine's in April, 1989, William Metcalf, Jr., the CEO of the company that is now known as the New Orleans Publishing Group, offered me the job as Associate Publisher/Editor of one of his recent acquisitions, *New Orleans Magazine*. A month later the new chapter had begun.

A year earlier, "I Never Danced With An Eggplant (On A Streetcar Before): Chronicles of Life and Adventures in New Orleans" had been released. The book consisted of a selection of my columns, collectively written under the heading of "Streetcar," which had been published during the seven years I served as associate editor and then as editor at *Gambit* newspaper. There are several things, in addition to memories, a person takes with him when changing jobs: personal books, pictures, phone listings, curios and, in my case, "Streetcar." The column had a new home in the back page of *New Orleans Magazine*.

This book is a collection of "Streetcar" columns written during my years to date at *New Orleans Magazine*. Mechanically, the change from a newsprint publication to a glossy magazine was enormous. Mentally, it was even greater. The timing was different. Not only was the shift from a weekly to a monthly but, because of production demands, the magazine had deadlines much further in advance of publication. When I began writing "Streetcar" for the magazine I was at first thrown by not always being able to be current. It took me several issues to become comfortable with my style. The breakthrough came when I rediscovered what I had known all along: "Streetcar" was about the everyday adventures and curiosities in New Orleans. There is no deadline urgency to pondering such concerns as the New Orleans summer, the anxieties of wearing a white suit, or what to do with too many bananas. Sure, I might be writing a column with a Christmas theme during Halloween week and writing about Mardi Gras during Christmas but at least I was able to live the city's annual life cycle twice: once to meet the early deadline, once for the actual experience. By late '89 I felt that "Streetcar" had again found its proper voice.

"Streetcar" is and has been about New Orleans. Even the occasional columns that tell about a travel experience relate back to this city which, after all, is the center of the universe — according to reliable sources. Loving New Orleans can sometimes be a torturous relationship, and there have been times when I must admit to having felt battered by the liaison. Recent years have been tough on the city and those who cherish it: the economy, crime, divisiveness — they have been potshots at the public confidence.

New Orleans should never be loved blindly. Those of us who choose to write about it should never become so immersed in its admittedly delightful quirks that we forget that this is a real city with real people facing real challenges. But perhaps it is those quirks that make the task of facing the reality a bit more palatable. New Orleanians face the problems of modern life, but at least while they do there is a hint of jasmine in the air.

This book is about the little things that are part of the New Orleans experience. When a streetcar reaches the end of its line, it can be reversed to travel back in the opposite direction. As one trip ends another begins, and though the routes remain the same there are always new things to behold and stories to tell along the way.

— *Errol Laborde*

ABOUT THE TITLE

Admittedly, "The Buzzard Wore A Tutu" is not an everyday sort of observation, but then New Orleans is not an everyday sort of city. The title is in reference to a group of men known as the Jefferson City Buzzards. The organization, which is more than a century old, was formed in uptown New Orleans in an area known as Jefferson City. There were once several slaughterhouses in the area so an occasional buzzard could be seen circling above, hence the inspiration for the group's name.

There are two days a year when the Jefferson City Buzzards can be spotted, not flying but marching, or perhaps staggering. One of those days is Mardi Gras when the Buzzards, in fine costumes, make their way along St. Charles Avenue en route to downtown ahead of the Zulu and Rex parades. They are accompanied by a jazz band.

Romping down the street requires some conditioning so the Buzzards annually have a warm-up procession on the third Sunday before Mardi Gras. For this event the gentlemen traditionally wear dresses and similar garb, including a tutu or two. So that they will not dehydrate in training, there are several bar stops along their path, including a refueling at Franky & Johnny's, an uptown seafood restaurant and bar. It is there that the Buzzards happen to meet another Carnival group, the Phunny Phorty Phellows, who on that day are having their annual crawfish party. In one of the most solemn moments of Carnival, the Phellows feed the Buzzards, many of whom have lost their glow by that point because of smeared mascara. Frequently the offering is leftover potatoes or ears of corn that were boiled with the crawfish. After the ceremony, and a few shots of beer, the Buzzards stagger on, continuing to fine tune the choreography for their Mardi Gras march.

Because they epitomize the spirit and individuality of New Orleans, the Buzzards seemed like the right image for the book's title. It might be said that a buzzard in a tutu isn't always a very pretty sight, but it sure knows how to have fun.

ACKNOWLEDGMENT

A book is the product of many minds. Such is true with this publication. Thanks begin with my wife, Peggy Scott Laborde, whose gentle urging and strong support made this publication possible.

Through the years there have been two names attached to "Streetcar," mine and artist Arthur Nead's. His skilled and insightful illustrations once again grace this book and once again, I am reluctant to admit, are likely the real attraction of "Streetcar."

There would be no "Streetcar" were it not for *New Orleans Magazine* and the magazine might not have survived were it not for Bill Metcalf. This book is in many ways a tribute to him and to the staff of the magazine who have nurtured, proofed, corrected and cared for the column through the years.

Susan Adamo had the demanding and lonely task of copy editing this book. Her insights and encouragement have added much to it.

Carole Rike and her gang at Word Catering not only added their professional expertise but were fun to work with.

And special thanks go to Sheila Bosworth, one of the city's premiere novelists, for her thoughtful Foreword.

Thanks to all of you. Let's do it again.

DEDICATION

To my parents, Ellis and Rena Laborde,
for their support, for having had a son and for having
had the wisdom to raise him in New Orleans.

IN MEMORY OF

GEORGE HERGET
1936-1994
BOOKSELLER EXTRAORDINAIRE

There would be no point in writing if someone did not
care for books, new and old. Printed words survived
and prospered because George Herget cared, and
because so many people cared about him.

TROPICAL NEW ORLEANS

BANANAS

This year I had my second straight banana crop. Not only that, but I doubled last year's harvest.

Banana trees have always been a part of the New Orleans landscape, but I've never known the local trees to bear so many real yellow, edible, actual bananas. "We're a little bit too far north," I've always been told. Well, the tree we inherited when we bought our house three years ago apparently has no sense of geography. Last year a

huge banana bunch sprouted from one of its limbs. I had to learn some of the basics of banana horticulture. When the banana bunch, which was still green, seemed fully developed I whacked off the purple bulb at the end that dangled from the bottom of the bunch. That, I was told, would prevent the nutrients from being diverted from the bananas. It must have worked, because within the next couple of weeks the bananas gradually began turning the desired yellow.

It was a bountiful bunch . . . perhaps a bit too bountiful, because a problem arose: what to do with a hundred or so perishable bananas? The obvious answer was to give them away, but these are not the type of bananas that Americans are used to. What's sold in supermarkets is probably some hybrid developed by German scientists in Brazil, whose mission it was to breed a banana that could survive the trip from the islands to the states, yet still be sliceable for corn flakes.

By contrast, what grew on my tree barely made the trip from the backyard to the kitchen before the peel started to turn brown. The shape was a bit different, too. Mine were a little shorter but a lot plumper than what mainlanders are used to. But what the homegrown bananas lacked in beauty they made up for in taste, fuller and richer than the store-bought kind. These, I surmise, are what bananas really tasted like when eaten fresh from the tree, rather than from off the counter, back in the days B.C. . . . Before Chiquita.

Luckily we had a Jamaican banana recipe book on hand, so I tried a recipe for banana jam. Unfortunately, the person who wrote the book must have been the same person who writes V.C.R. programming instructions. Some steps to the process seemed to be missing. The good news is I believe everyone who tried the jam seems to have survived.

Another rule to successful banana farming is to chop down the limb which bore the bunch. Having done its job once, the limb will never provide more fruit. So, if one rewards the limb's efforts with demolition, the tree's fickle nutrients can be directed to a new, more fertile limb. It worked. This year there were two bunches on my tree.

When the time was right, I whacked off the stem with the bulb (there's a lot of whacking involved in banana farming) and, as though by command, the bananas began to yellow. Only this year the bananas were so big, and the bunches were so heavy, that each bunch actually broke the limb from which it was hanging. Approximately 200 bananas crashed onto the grass.

This year, too, I was wiser about what to do with all those bananas. From the cookbook came somewhat workable recipes for banana chicken curry and banana custard. Those accounted for about six of the bananas. The other 194 or so became part of an experiment. Bananas, we were told, could be frozen. So we made a vat of banana mush and squeezed some lemon juice into it, supposedly preserving the color. We then spooned globs of the mush into freezer bags, wrapped the bags in foil, which is supposed to help prevent freezer burn, and placed the bags in the freezer. Now we have frozen banana mush for the whole year.

Why we would want it is another question. The simplest answer is that of the mountain climber who explained why he wanted to scale Mt. Everest . . . "because it's there." So, too, are the bananas.

A reason the fruit matured during the last couple of summers was because the last two winters were mild. One hard freeze this winter could knock out next year's crop. Depending on the weather, it might be years before the local trees bear fruit again. But there will be those occasions for warm banana bread or a cold banana daiquiri. To most people all bananas taste the same, but there is something special about produce when you know it's from your soil and that its cultivation is due in part to your well-timed whacks. But what if this winter is mild and there are 400 bananas next year? Somehow I will find something to do with them. Because they will be there.

ADVENTURES WITH A WHITE SUIT

This Easter Sunday will be the fifth anniversary of the first time I wore my white suit. That milestone is momentous to me because, after the first time I wore it, I didn't think I would be wearing it for too many more Easters.

I had always craved a white suit as a cultural curiosity. Every tribe has its costumes, and for the tribe of New Orleans men working downtown, the white suit was the proper selection to be worn on those special occasions during the days between Easter and Labor Day when the semi-tropical climate is often humid. Mayors were inaugurated in white suits, the men of the big law firms wore them to their socials. Charcoal gray suits with pin stripes are universal, but a white suit identifies a person with his geography.

My craving for such a suit, however, was moderated by cost and lethargy about shopping. Then in early '89 something happened which prompted the purchase. It was a sad announcement that Terry &

Juden, a classic long-time downtown men's store, was closing. In another era, the gentlemen of downtown got their suits at Terry & Juden, their shoes at Pokorny's and their Panamas at Meyer the Hatter, all within a few blocks of each other. That era was ending, but there would be a sale before the doors closed for good.

Prices were slashed, including those for a few remaining white suits sold off the rack, no longer with the benefit of the store's tailor to make them fit just right. The label inside said: "Terry & Juden, for 100 years in New Orleans." Its century was ending.

Making my suit fit required some work. The sleeves were too long and the pants needed hemming. The tailor at a rival store promised that the suit would be ready in two weeks, in plenty of time for Easter.

That Easter Sunday the suit made its debut at one of those restaurant brunches in the French Quarter. I was proud to be wearing it, but as I started to eat I discovered there is one problem with white suits: they are so — white. During the entire meal I was sensitive to the suit. Each of my movements was accompanied by an internal alarm cautioning me to make sure my sleeves didn't land in a sauce or that nothing squirted in my direction. White suits keep no secrets; anything that lands on them, from flecks to smears, is easily apparent. Sauce on the pasta? No thanks, I'm wearing a white suit. A topping for the dessert? You've got to be kidding. And, please, no French bread, too many crumbs. The best approach to dining while wearing a white suit is to fast.

Since that day I have worn the suit an average of twice a year: Easter and one other miscellaneous occasion. I have discovered the best situation for wearing such a suit is an event in which the wearer does not have to touch anything or be touched, where there are no waiters with trays who might spill things. It is a great suit to wear while standing stationary, as long as you contain movement to a minimum.

I discovered last Summer some people are much more at ease in a white suit than I. I was invited to an uptown wedding for which there was an outdoor reception at a country club. All the men were dressed in white except for me. I was not in the proper color because (one) I didn't know better, and (two) I had already reached the quota of two white suit wearings for the year. I did feel sort of like the fudge in the ripple, and I was in awe of the other men who did not seem to be at all intimidated by their suits. They moved, talked, ate and drank freely as though their suits were protected with Scotchguard. Uptowners, I thought, have certain skills I have yet to master.

I do know that the white suit season is back and that, in this my suit's fifth year, it is time for me to try to loosen up. I should try to be more daring while wearing it this year. If others can do it so can I. This Easter I might even go for the dessert — as long as it's vanilla.

WHITE SUITS: THE SEQUEL

When we left off, this column had commented about the plight of the New Orleans male when it comes to wearing a local standard, the white suit. We noted that white suits, properly worn between Easter and Labor Day, have been the uniform of uptown businessmen, attorneys, bon vivants and politicians during the season. It also made note that the suits can drive a person crazy because they get dirty so easily — cocktailsauceaphobia, it might be called.

Response has been great, including that of a certain uptowner who admits to being converted to the suits only after having attended a summer uptown wedding a decade or so ago. He had decided to wear tan poplin that day. All the other men were in white. Normally, he says, he is not one to follow fashion statements, a reaction against his days of wearing uniforms in the Navy, but on this issue he has preferred to join the flock just because it makes him feel more comfortable, or perhaps less conspicuous. In doing so he has become an observer of white suit etiquette. We'll call him Deep Pocket.

According to Deep, there are certain situations in which the details of what to wear with a white suit are very rigid. If, for example, a man is going to a summer function at either the Orleans Club or The New Orleans Country Club (better known in knowing circles as "*The* Country Club") the proper accoutrement is a white shirt (never one that is colored) along with black socks, shoes and belt. The tie, Deep said, must be dignified, no plaids, none of the bold, new-fangled stuff. If a person really wants to express his individuality, he is allowed a choice between his shirt collar being button-down or plain.

I asked Deep if there was any occasion when a colored shirt was appropriate with a white suit. "At a barbecue," he teased. He then confessed that he has worn color with his white suit at Easter brunches and that the combination might be okay for certain more informal yard parties. "But," he cautioned, "be sure of yourself."

Deep revealed that he personally does not like the idea of white shirts with a white suit. "Nothing looks worse," he says, "because the suits themselves differ in their degree of whiteness. The whitest were the classic 100 percent linen suits which were once more commonly worn. They are hard to keep clean and hard to maintain. "A person didn't look right in them unless the suit was slightly rumpled," Deep recalled. People would have to boil the suits to clean them." Mr. Pocket whispered that his own preference is for a suit made partially with "good ol' fashion polyester."

Modern times have raised some new questions about white suit etiquette. For example, there are some people who regularly wear white suits to the Zoo-To-Do even though the event is listed as being "black tie." Deep recalled that one year he went up to someone he knew at the event who was wearing a white suit and chided him. "But," the acquaintance answered, "my tie is black." An added confusion is that the term "black tie" is usually taken to mean that a tuxedo should be worn, but the ties which are worn with tuxedos nowadays are more often not black. This, then, is the question for the 90's: Which is more appropriate at a New Orleans summer black tie event, to wear a white suit with a black tie or to dress in what is considered as a black tie but to have a tie that might not be black? It will be a difficult decade.

White bucks, according to Deep Pockets, are seldom the appropriate shoes to wear with white suits, except perhaps for those rare occasions (see above) when a colored shirt is okay. This particular rule, incidentally, suits me fine because I don't have white bucks, but I do have black shoes. As for a hat, there can only be one answer — a panama. That too is all right with me since I already have one, even though my preference is for a baseball cap, but that might be pushing things too far. A person might see his oyster patty taken away.

Since Easter is a movable feast, the white suit season can vary. Next year, for example, Easter will be eight days earlier than it was this year. That means that there will be an extra week and a day to worry about stains. In any season, the demands on those suits worn by men whose social card is full can be great. On the day the season ends, it is time for the cleaners to get busy. That's why they call it Labor Day.

THE HEAT

Heat is a fickle giant. It torments and teases the city, yet it wants to hug, being so passionate in its embrace that it can be smothering.

These are the days when the summer sun takes aim. Its scattershot blasts strike other places as well, of course, but few towns are as defined by the heat as is New Orleans. The soft and dreamy images of the city — the verandas, the shade of the oaks and the golden rains, the breezy palms, the lazy ceiling fans trying to churn a breeze — all are a part of the city trying to address the heat. In return, the heat not only addresses the city but dresses it. Mayors are inaugurated, as summer nears, dressed in traditional white, just as the gentleman of the law firms have dressed for their summer socials. Haspel suits, once made in New Orleans, were designed to be light so as to be cool.

That pursuit of things cool is fueled by the heat as though powered by its steam, yet it is the steam that hastens the pursuit. If the weather were merely hot, the season would be tolerable, but it is the humidity —

the heat's coat of oven-baked moisture — that slows the pace, and occasionally the spirit. Not so much of the spirit, however, to have stifled the sort of inventiveness triggered by the threat. Thus was it from New Orleans, the city that converted street music into jazz, that came the world's best mass-produced machines with the endearing purpose of changing ice into snow — cold, soft snow, gushing from the mouth of an "Ortolano SnoWizard," made on Magazine Street, or an "Eisenmann Fluffy Ice," made on St. Claude. The new snow would be sprayed into Dixie Cups then splashed with syrups and lanced with a straw and spoon to complete the perfect snowball, the native remedy for an epidemic of the heat.

But while the snowball machines merely attempt to soothe the heat, another invention mercilessly tries to eradicate it, and in doing so disrupts the natural order — just as a pesticide kills the bugs but poisons the streams as well. While the air conditioner boxed out the heat, in doing so it has made useless all the graceful remedies. Had New Orleans first flowered in the era of the air conditioner, there would be no need for wide galleries in our architecture or high ceilings or louvered windows or green shutters or ceiling fans stirring a jasmine-scented breeze. There would be no need for oak-lined streets or a breezy sea wall. The people could have stayed cool by staying concealed so as to contain the central air. We would not have needed the amenities built to combat the heat, and we would have lost the artistry in their design.

Curiously, the effort to combat the heat has evolved its own architecture as well — creating an inside for things that naturally belong outdoors. An old-timer once recalled to me that people used to spend their summer evenings watching minor league baseball at Pelican Stadium because it was a way to keep cool, as though the swatting of the bats created its own breeze. Now there is no baseball team in New Orleans but there is a ball park, one with a roof and with central air. The Superdome's soft arc stands in the skyline like a monument to having thrown nature a curve.

Yet nothing made by man can fully beat the heat, which takes its revenge in other ways. The heat steams the Gulf of Mexico, making it angry enough to raise a protest of storms. The mildest of those are the summer rains which are out to get those who are on the way to their air-conditioned hideouts. The meanest are the tropical storms and hurricanes, stopping things in their tracks as they make their own. The rains can seep through doorways, the winds can disrupt electric power and in doing so both ridicule and make temporarily useless those places sealed for air conditioning. Even on its best behavior, the heat teases of its potential: in the quiet of warm summer nights, the occasional rumble and flash in the distant sky of heat lightning. It is lightning flickering over a city where the night moods are affected by the deep warmth. The temperature incubates the mosquito ponds, their raiders being even more aggravation for those whose tempers are already triggered by the thermometer. The warm stickiness creates crime and passion yet also romantic images. And New Orleans, like the oak, both tolerates and thrives on the weather; for in nature, as in politics and business, those who survive are those who are best able to take the heat.

CARNIVAL

THE MYSTERY MASKERS
OF TWELFTH NIGHT

There's a mysterious ritual that I have been witness to on the evening of the last few Twelfth Nights, during the hours when Christmas segues into the carnival season. By then, all the lords have leaped and the pipers have piped. The main characters at this point are three men-a-masking.

It all begins at the Willow Street streetcar barn. A group, which borrows its name from a 19th century carnival organization, the Phorty Phunny Phellows, gathers in a hired streetcar to ride the rails, announcing the new season's arrival. I've been able to tag along, which has put me in the right place at the right time to notice three mysterious masked figures who assemble across the street from the car barn. A typical costume for each is a trench coat, a hat, and a traditional expressionless, full-face mask like those worn in some of the older carnival organizations. These characters carry signs, each one a gentle statement on carnival. "Beau Done the Best He Could," one sign said last year in reference to Beau Bassich, the chairman of the city's Mardi Gras coordinating committee. (Bassich tried to calm tensions during the carnival ordinance controversy.) "Arthur Hardy Discriminates against the Krewe of Lake Catherine," another sign said, a teasing reference to the carnival guidebook publisher overlooking an unknown parade.

But a sign that I look for the most has yet to be shown . . . the one that would give some indication about who the three are. No one knows. Each year we talk to them but their voices are not familiar. We try to see something we recognize in their eyes, peering through the masks. Nothing. There isn't anything about their presence that provides information about them. We're like the townspeople in a western movie asking, "Who are those masked men?"

By now their pattern has become predictable. When the streetcar leaves the barn, so do they. They will appear again, standing on the neutral ground, usually in the vicinity of Napoleon Avenue. There they display some new signs as the streetcar rolls by. The riders wave to them, but the masked faces merely stare — expressionless.

On some Twelfth Night evenings the group has appeared again somewhere along Carondelet Street. One definite stopping point, however, is Gallier Hall. By the evening of Twelfth Night the reviewing stands for the carnival season have already been erected. In the weeks ahead, the monarchs of Carnival will be toasted at Gallier Hall as they lead their parades along the Avenue. For the parades of Bacchus and Endymion, and when Zulu and Rex pass on Mardi Gras, the streets and stands will be packed with revelers. But these first hours of the carnival season are like the stream in Minnesota where the Mississippi begins — over time and distance a trickle becomes a great river. In the dark solitude of Gallier Hall on the last day of Christmas the trickle begins. There the mystery maskers display still more signs, and there they present the streetcar riders with a gift. One year the present was a videotape of the maskers' appearance the year before (minus any indication of who they might be); another year it was what amounted to a Carnival survival kit, including a Mrs. Drake's sandwich and a Barq's. The threesome, in return, is toasted by the Phellows. The evening is the maskers' last appearance . . . until the next Twelfth Night. After Gallier Hall, they disappear into the mist and reality.

I am perplexed by the three. My curiosity wants to know who they really are — but my sentimentality doesn't. They typify more of the spirit of Carnival than many of the tired parades that roll past Gallier Hall. There's not enough mystery and humor left in Carnival, except for on the last day of Christmas when three witty and wise men bear gifts. To know who they are might break the spell.

Carnival, I fear, is in trouble. It is gradually being taken over by people who are in it just to make a buck. But as the streetcar heads back to Willow Street each Twelfth Night, I know that somewhere in the city the spirit lives. Outwardly their masks show no expression, but certainly they must be smiling on the inside.

WHATEVER HAPPENED TO MARDI GRAS NIGHT?

Maybe it's because I write for a living, but I really feel a need for punctuation marks!!! I expect them at the end of a sentence, which is normal, but I also expect them in life, which may not be so normal. As someone who cares deeply about Carnival, one of the moments I enjoyed most was the visualization of the punctuation marks that came in the last hours of the season — the rituals that closed Carnival. Now those rituals are gone and Carnival has no ending: it's just a participle dangling into Ash Wednesday.

By Mardi Gras evening, about the only people still left downtown were the tourists, the crazies and the Carnival buffs. They formed the crowd that watched the Mystik Krewe of Comus roll through the streets. To me it was a magnificent moment, as though Carnival's senior Krewe had the prerogative to snuff out the candles for another season. Carnival is so delicate, there is so much that could go wrong on the streets, that I always felt some relief when the last Comus float rolled by. Carnival had survived another year, and this city, often maligned, though nevertheless great, had again proven itself able to safely host something no other city could.

Within the ritual of watching Comus, which first paraded in 1857, there was a sub-ritual that began in 1980. A year earlier there had been no parades within the city limits because of a police strike. Dutch Morial, then mayor, and the cops were in a standoff. The Krewes, and increasingly the public, stood behind the mayor. It was a bitter, divisive Carnival season.

That made the moment all the more special on the evening of Mardi Gras 1980, when the lead units of the Comus parade reached Gallier Hall. Morial was there to exchange toasts with Comus, but there was also another very special salute to be made. At the head of the parade was a platoon of police, each in their dress blues. Champagne glasses were passed out so the mayor and the cops could toast each other. The toast ended, in Mardi Gras fashion, with the glasses dropped, shattering on the ground. Another tradition was born. Each year after that, on Mardi Gras night, the mayor and the police, in the presence of Comus, would honor each other. For one loving moment, civic authority, symbolic authority and the cops on the beat celebrated together. Now that, too, doesn't happen anymore.

By tradition, Carnival ended when Rex left his Carnival ball, near midnight, to meet Comus at his. The "Meeting of the Courts" was annually broadcast by WDSU-TV. By the standards of the MTV generation, it was boring television but its numbing quality was suited for the closing moments of the Carnival season. We always toasted the meeting with champagne — Carnival's last bit of celebration. The broadcast has stopped as well.

I'm not sure when or where Mardi Gras ends now. Maybe it's when the last honking vehicle from the truck parade turns off the route; or maybe it's when the police in the Quarter begin nudging loiterers to move on. Or it could simply be when the hands on the Cathedral's clock meet at XII. None present much of a public spectacle.

Now it's just the tourists and crazies downtown on Mardi Gras night. The buffs have nowhere to go. And to everyone else it is just another Tuesday night. Carnival's ending is left to the mind and soul. The emptiness reigns.

We learn from what is lost. Things just don't seem right without the proper punctuation at the end.

Do they —

ABALONE STEAK!

Even as I write this I can still hear in my mind the vendor's strange yell, "Abalone Steak! Abalone Steak!" This particular Carnival parade season had gotten off to an unusual start.

Spring's arrival is registered in different ways in different places. To me, the introduction to the oncoming season, even when the weather doesn't cooperate, has always been what I call, "Carrollton Sunday." That's the day when the Krewe of Carrollton marches up Canal Street through Mid-City towards downtown. For generations of people, the Carrollton parade, held on the first Sunday of the parade season, is their first annual brush with Mardi Gras. Carrollton Sunday is when New Orleanians leave their winter coops to experience once again the streets and open spaces.

That's what I was doing on that day a couple of years ago. For those who live near the route, the parade's coming is a social event. It's common to mill about on the neutral ground long before the parade's arrival. Part of the scene is the vendors who have commandeered shopping carts, from which they sell Carnival-type food . . . peanuts and candied apples, cotton candy or caramel popcorn.

But abalone steak? That was what I heard as the vendor approached.

My only previous experience with abalone was in California. The mollusks are plentiful there. They are generally found clinging to rocks in the vicinity of the bays. In taste and texture they resemble scallops. The size is similar, too. They are relatively small, hardly large enough to carve a good chop from, much less a steak. But perhaps some crazed scientist at Berkeley had developed a way to inject the abalone with steroids so they would grow to a size suitable for butchering. If so, would the cut be a filet or a porterhouse? If served on a bun, should they be splashed with steak sauce or tartar sauce? This could very well be a new adventure in dining.

Sirens interrupted the vendor's strange yell — the parade was approaching. So it wasn't until after the Krewe of Carrollton had passed, during a lull before the arrival of Okeanos, the parade that used to follow Carrollton, that I again heard the cry, "Abalone Steak! Abalone Steak!"

Up to this point, I hadn't taken the yell seriously. I had just assumed I had misunderstood what the vendor, a young woman, was saying. But then a friend heard the yell too, turned to me and asked, "Did she say abalone steak!?" This culinary question could no longer be ignored.

We approached the vendor. "Excuse me," I asked, "did you say 'abalone steak'?"

"What?" the vendor responded.

"Abalone steak," I repeated. "Are you selling abalone steak?" There was a blank look on her face. Then she shook her head, reached into the basket, pulled out the items she was hawking and pronounced the words slowly, "apple-on-a-stick, apple-on-a-stick."

We all laughed. It was just as well that she wasn't selling abalone steak, because she wasn't offering side orders of rice pilaf.

There is a postscript to this story. Last year I was in San Francisco, and one evening we had dinner at one of those restaurants at Fisherman's Wharf. I was examining the menu when I was suddenly stunned by what I saw. There was a seafood item called "Scalone Steak." Scallops and abalone were blended and pressed together to form a large steak-sized patty, which was deep-fried. It was served with a baked potato. That's what I ordered. It was great. I thought about that vendor at the Carrollton parade. On the plate before me was a steak that was at least half abalone.

We didn't have dessert, but we might have if only the menu had had what I wanted.

Unfortunately, nowhere was there a listing for apple-on-a-stick.

DUCKS

DINNER WITH THE DUCKS

By intention, if not design, this was supposed to be one of those quiet, after-work dinners with the objective of taking advantage of the extra hours of summer sun. After a stop to pick up a modest meal of a sandwich and a bag of Zapp's potato chips I parked near the peristyle, that open building with the Greek columns near the City Park tennis courts, and headed for a bench alongside the lagoon.

My knowledge of telepathy among birds is nil but I know enough to know when there is a lot of communicating going on, and that is what was happening when I approached the park bench as ducks of all sorts, dozens of ducks, brown and white, big and little, suddenly emerged running towards me. From a duck's view there was hardly anything about my possessions to suggest a great bounty. I carried only a small paper bag with the food in it and a soft drink cup, hardly enough for a feast for a flock. Something about me made them assume that there was more than there actually was. Meanwhile, other people sitting on other benches grinned at my predicament. A couple walked by of which the he in the group smiled and observed, "you've got a lot of ducks there." I hadn't noticed.

In fact, the number was growing in the same way that a sudden crowd of humans arouses the curiosity of other humans who join the crowd, which in turn attracts even more. At this rate of mathematical progression I would have every duck in the continent eyeing my Zapp's within a half-hour.

This is when I had to make some hard decisions. I would have gladly shared a few morsels with the birds except, given the determined looks on their faces, I knew that would be a mistake. One crumb would cause a panic and the word of food would be spread to everything in the sky. I could imagine hawks and eagles circling above. So my strategy was two-fold: first try to shoo them away. They barely budged, sensing, correctly I guess, that I was no threat. All that was left was step two, which was to ignore them and hope they would be driven away by sheer boredom. So I munched on the sandwich while trying to be as oblivious as possible to 200 eyes encircling me, watching every move I made. To show them I didn't care I stared at the lagoon where two swans, totally uninterested in me, glided by. I gained a new respect for swans that moment, not as much for their beauty as for their politeness. In the school of bird etiquette I could just imagine some teacher bird scolding a class full of ducks saying, "look at the swans, you don't see *them* begging, do you?"

Suddenly the tranquillity of the lagoon was broken by two mallards flying in tandem, like the Navy's Blue Angels, coming in for a landing. They splashed down about twenty yards away but then immediately ran toward me as though they had been notified by ground control. Now there were four extra eyes staring. At this point it seemed that the scene was about as congested as possible but then it got worse. From somewhere behind me there was the sound of a loud honking noise moving in my direction. As the ducks must have been thinking, so was I: "The goose is coming."

For the record, a goose does not walk with a goose step; instead, it waddles with more of an elephant walk. This big bird came up to me even closer than the ducks dared and stared and honked without mercy. The ducks began their noise, too, creating a scene that, were it not for the absence of tin cups, would have seemed like a prison riot.

This might have gone on forever except that God intervened and sent a human family in the distance in which the momma carried a bag of popcorn. Word quickly spread among the birds, most of whom, including the goose, waddled away. Which is what I did also, heading for home where there is generally a cat begging for milk on the front porch who at least has the grace not to bring the gang with him.

As seems to be necessary for stories involving animals, there was a lesson to be learned from all this. A week later, I went back to the same site carrying no more than the same sized meal that I had the previous time. A few ducks spotted me but none came running. They just went about the business of being ducks. Feeling less threatened, I was able to toss in the lagoon some pieces of bread to which two hatchlings raced. I could toss at random to the passing ducks, some of whom were merely waddling by. There was also a few pieces for the goose, who made a brief but restrained appearance. Perhaps the birds had learned what must be true for all of life, and that is that those who are best able to gather the bread are those who don't travel with the flock.

THE DUCKS
OF BREAKWATER DRIVE

There is a row of boat houses along Breakwater Drive. As far as I know, there are no permanent residents in those houses, but there are regular dwellers along the drive, and they have taken to the neighborhood like ducks to water. In fact, they are ducks, a colony of them — mostly mallards but with a few park-variety white ducks and a goose or two to keep the neighborhood mixed.

On most days the ducks exist on what is about as idyllic a setting as possible. Breakwater Drive is the finger of land that juts into Lake Pontchartrain, across the harbor from the Southern Yacht Club. The strip acts as a barrier that stops the lake's wave action on one side, thus providing a quiet harbor on the other. This is where the ducks hang out, right along the curve where they bob on the gentle water, which on good days is disturbed only by the sailboats gliding to and from the lake. They are pampered birds who are no doubt amused by that species known as humans, who seem to have an uncontrollable urge to feed them. Throughout the day old men whose retirement ritual includes tossing bread and popcorn to the ducks make their visit. People who are fishing off of the banks do the same. And then there are the up-and-coming generations, toddlers whose parents stand by coaching them to fling pieces of feed into the water.

Parenthood is something that the ducks can relate to because there is a lot of parenting going on. There is now a school of brown ducklings providing more mouths for the willing humans to feed.

That's what it's like on the good days, and there are plenty of them, but then there are the times when it gets too wet, even for ducks. That happened during the recent rainy spell when there was too much water for even a lake to contain. Day after day the rain fell and the water level climbed — foul weather not fit for a fowl. The road was covered with water in most spots and the warm pieces of riprap, broken bits of concrete placed near the water as a barrier, were slippery wet. It rained so hard for so long that nothing was the same anymore. The quiet harbor was gurgling with overflow, water was being pitched down the riprap from the lake side of the peninsula. The water may have fallen easily off the ducks' backs, but it was, nevertheless, water that was rising.

There was no sign of the ducklings who were probably hurried into crevices within the riprap slabs clumped along the bank. Two adult ducks were heading into one opening in the rock pile at the same time and bumped into each other. It may be that most of the world's conflicts can be attributed to turf battles — that's true of politics, the office, even the home; and it's true of ducks running for cover. Once, in one of those nearby Breakwater Drive boat houses, some politicians met to agree to support a particular councilman to fill a vacancy in the mayor's office. The meeting fell apart, however, when the opposing councilman showed up to stake his claim to the political turf. In a different world, though on the same street, life's battles continue. The two ducks battled each other for the spot in the riprap, one pecking at the other's neck until he was driven away. Another turf battle fought along Breakwater Drive.

Crisis can create conflict but it can also stir creativity. Ducks may be the most versatile of all creatures, being the only ones that can fly, swim and walk. But they seem to be the happiest when they are merely bobbing on still water. In pursuit of that happiness some of the birds found relief. With water overflowing, some of the low spots on the land that would ordinarily become mere puddles were filled high enough and wide enough to serve as instant ponds. While the sea splashed violently from either side of the breakwater, those ducks rested on their newly found harbor.

A few days later that puddle would be dry. The rain had stopped, the lake had receded. The real harbor was quiet enough for the ducks to return to their business of being ducks. The ducklings were taking a dip, again sharing the pool with the passing sailboats. The spot in the slabs over which there had been a battle was now meaningless. When the sky is clear there is turf enough for everyone. Life continued along Breakwater Drive, but now its inhabitants were wiser in their ability to seek calm waters amidst a storm.

FOLKS

THE MAN IN THE PARK

As soon as she spotted Malcom sitting on the park bench, the girl broke away from her date. She ran behind the bench and put her arm around the man. Meanwhile her date collected evidence of this alienation of affections by taking a photograph of the woman and Malcom together.

Moments later another couple walked by. Again, the woman of the pair was drawn to Malcom. And again the male took a picture, except he seemed to be more in compliance since he actually urged the woman to embrace Malcom. But the woman resisted, perhaps not wanting to seem too forward. She merely rubbed Malcom on the head while he sat quietly.

There are those who say that Malcom is a bit stiff; nevertheless, his charm comes from the liveliness in his presence. He lives on because he is lifelike. And he steals hearts because he is easy to touch, and in doing so one can easily be touched by him.

By now those lifelike street scene sculptures are becoming common in public places. There are already a few human-sized butchers and bakers in the French Market and there is the figure of a policeman standing at the ground level of the Energy Centre. The first I ever saw was in Boston, where I, too, posed for a camera alongside the image of a former Boston machine-era politician.

And, like a machine, there seems to be something mechanical, if not downright magical, about the appeal of pretend-people to real people. In few places does that magic exude as it does for the figure of Malcom Woldenberg seated in the park named after him located along the riverfront next to the aquarium.

It is an appropriate setting because although Woldenberg, who founded a liquor company , lived a private life, his statue located on the pathway of all those walking along the riverfront, exists as though in a goldfish bowl.

Sharing the bench with Woldenberg is the figure of a boy. The youngster seems to be listening to the older man, who is facing in his direction and whose right palm is turned up as though trying to make a point. It is as though an exchange of wisdom, once spoken, was suddenly frozen in time. Perhaps in the process a device was implanted in the sculptures, a device with a magnetic pull on the human heart: A man was walking along the park's path. Suddenly he deviated from his track, stopped to pat Woldenberg's head, then moved on. The entire gesture seemed almost unconscious. He was like a glider aloft suddenly pushed toward a cloud by a gust of wind before regaining its course.

And it continues that way throughout the day, every day. A group of teenagers walked by who felt compelled to pose. One of the girls giggled incessantly as she sat atop Woldenberg's shoulders. For the sake of the inevitable photograph, one of the teenagers situated a pair of sunglasses on the boy statue as though to make him resemble the bespectacled Woldenberg. Others posed more reverently. Through it all Woldenberg never once flinched. Perhaps he was mesmerized by the view.

From where Mr. Woldenberg sits, the Canal Street ferry can be seen making its trips back and forth across the nation's spine. Perhaps Woldenberg is pointing out to the boy that the ferry doesn't really propel itself forward but swings sideways, making a gentle s-shaped glide to the opposite bank. Its waves are cut through by a huge, somber freighter carrying a Bahamian flag. Might the boy be wondering how anything so big can move so silently or why something that is comparatively smaller, such as a paddlewheeler carrying tourists as freight, can be so noisy? The guys who haul the cargo know no calliopes; they sway to the rhythm of the river. That rhythm provides the music for the grand water pageant taking place continuously along the Mississippi's deepest curve as ships and sailors pass each other. But somehow Mr. Woldenberg, sitting meekly and quietly, manages to compete for the attention.

Adding to the curiousness of it all is that those who gather around him to pat, stroke and hug him frequently feel compelled to read the accompanying inscription out loud to the rest of their entourage. So over and over, everyday, it is announced to friends by friends that the park is dedicated to Woldenberg, its benefactor, who "prospered in New Orleans and left a legacy of caring and of confidence in the city of New Orleans."

That message, as well as its subject, would probably go unnoticed were it chiseled into a granite base on which stood a traditional statue of the sort usually depicting generals and politicians and on which pigeons roost. If there is a lesson from all this, it may be that, for people as well as for sculptures, it is generally easier to be appreciated when you are down to earth rather than on a pedestal.

AL SCRAMUZZA ADIEU

It must have been the way that the planets were aligned on the day when he was born, but there are three things about Al Scramuzza that, when combined, make him a classic local character.

One is his name.

Another is his appearance, a tiny mustache beneath a notable nose.

And the third is the fact that the guy sold crawfish for a living. Take one away and it's not the same. There's nothing funny about a guy named Al Scramuzza who is, say, a U.S. attorney, an investment analyst or an insurance agent. Nor is there much color in a crawfish salesman with a mainstream name like Smith or Jones. And a more handsome Scramuzza just wouldn't have looked right in all those TV commercials. Al Scramuzza had it all — the name, the looks and the product.

Had his last name not been what it is, the region would have been deprived of his commercial jingle's rhyming scheme, in which one memorable line said, "Stay with Al Scramuzza and you'll never be a looza." Now I am worried. Scramuzza has closed his business. Since we will no longer be able to stay with Al Scramuzza, are we all therefore destined to be loozas? Just when things seemed to be getting better.

One day there should be a special spot in the Smithsonian for those classically American roadside businesses with names that suggest not just a place, but a territory. There are two such examples along Broad Street. One is on North Broad — the "Hub-cap King." If he is a king, then his place, filled with dented leftovers, must be a kingdom. Scramuzza was the other who, by contrast, was not a royalist, but rather played the populist. His place was not a kingdom, but a "Seafood City" over which we assume he was mayor for life.

His Honor was also the town physician, in one memorable TV commercial in which he assumed the role of the Crawfish Doctor. It was a noisy skit in which the prescription for whatever ailed folks was a batch of crawdads. Like Lourdes, Seafood City was a place people could visit to find the cure.

Visitors there could also find examples of art and letters which, if not worthy of a museum, were certainly worthy of a place where crawfish were sold. On one wall was a drawing entitled, "Sea Food City on Parade." Depicted in the scene were a shrimp, a crab and a crawfish, each playing a horn from which musical notes flowed. Behind them was a fish with a top hat playing a saxophone, carrying a second-line umbrella. It was a remarkable feat, especially for a fish. On another wall was a sign which proved that Scramuzza, like Shakespeare, knew how to play with puns: "Lookie Wit U Eyes and See Food City."

To Shakespeare, the crawfish business might have been much ado about nothing, but to Scramuzza it was his stage. And dare the bard ever achieve the honors bestowed upon the mudbug vendor. What higher plateau can man reach than having been depicted, as was Scramuzza one year, in the Endymion parade? The float, which honored local characters, featured Scramuzza's prominent proboscis. By contrast, what's so funny about a guy from England who just wrote plays for a living?

Now Scramuzza is living off past glory. He's retired. Just as small towns were once absorbed by expanding metropolises, the site of Seafood City will be part of a drugstore expansion. But don't cry for Scramuzza. Recently he stood outside his now closed building after just having bought his lunch at the neighboring grocery. Scramuzza said, while biting into his meal, that he was glad it was over. It was time to close. And just what does a guy who achieved immortality in the seafood business have for lunch? Liverwurst, of course.

Al Scramuzza is living the good life now. And whatever the future may bring, one truth remains — he will never be a looza.

BUSTER HOLMES

There are two things for which the river settlement of Ironton in Plaquemines Parish might be best noted. One is controversy; the other is Buster Holmes

The controversy was that Ironton, a black community in a parish once noted for its hostility to minorities, was one of the last places in the state to get running water.

Buster Holmes, by contrast, was not about controversy but rather goodwill.

As a teenager, Clarence "Buster" Holmes would move to the big city to the north, New Orleans, where he would enter the world of commerce by selling his own homemade sweet potato pies on the street. Eventually he would open a small business and develop a big reputation. Not bad for someone from a town so poor the only water that flowed was in the Mississippi.

Buster Holmes, who recently died at age 89, was best known for one of the things by which New Orleans is also best known — red beans and rice. His restaurant in the French Quarter was a beans emporium, known for its multicultural clientele decades before that adjective became chic. Truth is, other places may have had better red beans and rice, but no place sold them as inexpensively . . . and no place, no place in the world, had quite the down-home, funky mood that Buster Holmes' had. That's why his customer base included not only the hip and the adventurous looking for a cultural curiosity, but the poor and the hungry looking for survival.

Buster's had a simple interior. There were rows of long tables topped with bowls of butter to accompany the ever-present French bread. Depending on the day, there might have been some sort of greens — mustard or collard, whatever was available.

But red beans and rice were the staples. The beans and rice were cheap — sausage, pork chops, or fried fish was a bit extra. There was no symmetry to the dishes, no delicate balance of flavors or food groups. Any available chunk of meat was appropriate for plopping atop the beans. A person could get red beans with fried chicken at Buster's. That may have seemed heavy and uneven, but nowadays that sane combination is a dinner special at Popeye's.

I met Buster Holmes twice, and both times he seemed like a nice, soft-spoken man. What I remember most was his smile. It was big and gentle. He had lots to smile about. By his last years he had become a local icon. There were Buster Holmes T-shirts and even a fast food version of his place at the Jax Brewery food court. Given time, money and marketing help, he might have become the Colonel Sanders of red beans.

But the Buster Holmes who comes to mind was one I never knew. I once interviewed record producer Cosmio Matassa about his early days operating the studio where much of the city's rhythm and blues classics were recorded. The studio was on the corner of Rampart and Dumaine. Next door, on Dumaine, was Buster Holmes' original place. That's where the gang from the studio would eat. The mind wanders to envision Little Richard or Fats Domino wolfing down some of Buster's chow between takes. I asked Matassa if he realized back then the importance of the music he was recording. "No, " he said, "we just thought we were making a living." That's probably the way Holmes felt, too. He was just a guy cookin' beans for the guys who were makin' records. Nothing special. On neither side of the counter did the people realize they were making hits.

Holmes was always personally close to musicians, so much so that one of his favorite hangouts was the Palm Court Jazz Cafe on Decatur Street. The garlic chicken and the red beans served there are his recipes, as taught by Holmes. Nina Buck, the Palm Court's owner, recalls that whenever she offered Holmes a table for dinner he would say he preferred to be, "with his boys." He'd go to the kitchen and eat there.

Mardi Gras of this year now has extra meaning. There was a private party held in the Quarter, and Buster was asked to supervise the preparation of the red beans. Staff members from the Palm Court did the serving. It would be the last time Buster Holmes was present when his beans were dished out.

He was buried after a jazz funeral. The Algiers Brass Band was there. Greg Stafford and Milton Batiste also played. Tuba Fats looked on. In terms of mileage, Ironton wasn't far away. In terms of a life, it was in another world.

Buster Holmes had traveled far over a short distance. And along the way, didn't he ramble.

KING OF CAJUN

Somewhere above the field of the Jazz fest this month someone will begin playing a fiddle, and if the bow is directed properly, from that instrument will come the swaying sound of a song called "Jole Blon." Those in the crowd will start dancing, they can hardly avoid it when the song is played, since the rhythm has a way of causing people to move with it. Some will recognize the song as being the closest there is to a state anthem and certainly the most famous piece of Cajun music ever. Hardly anyone, I suspect, will know about Harry Choates, who made the song famous but whose own short life ended abruptly in a Texas jail.

Dance for Harry Choates. He knew fiddling better than he knew living, and it was the sounds from his fiddle that would last the longest.

It wasn't Choates who first recorded "Jole Blon;" that was done by Joseph Falcon, who was born near the Cajun town of Rayne. There were two great events in Louisiana in 1928, although at the time probably no one could grasp the lasting impact of either. Huey Long became governor after campaigning passionately to the little people and Joe Falcon recorded something called "Ma Blonde Est Partie" that touched the passions of those same people. The song, which became better known as "Jole Blon," was, as the story goes, written by Falcon's accordionist, Amidie Breaux, supposedly about his first wife who we could only assume, as the title suggests, was a pretty blonde. As the lyrics tell, the blonde's affections waned and in doing so created not only heartbreak but music:

Jole Blon, pretty girl,/Dear little one, pretty heart,
You left me to go away/With another, dear little one,
In the country of Louisiana/You poor one.

In the following year other groups, including the Hackberry Ramblers, would record their version of the song, but the decisive moment was in 1946 when Choates, a little-known Louisiana dance hall fiddler, recorded it for the Gold Star label in Houston, Texas. Initially there was no reaction to the record until a Houston disc jockey gave it a chance. The song caught on quickly, especially among Cajuns living near the Texas gulf, and then perhaps because of the novelty of the French lyrics backed by something close to a Texas swing sound, its popularity spread even further.

Choates never had another hit that big, but then he hardly had a chance. When he wasn't fiddling he was likely drinking, but bourbon and bowing didn't mix.

His last performance was at a dance hall in Austin, Texas. Back in Louisiana, July 14th is remembered by the French as Bastille day, the anniversary of the revolution that began with the storming of the Paris prison. But on that day in 1951 the singer of the most popular French Louisiana song went to jail. Choates was held on a warrant from Beaumont, Texas where he had been charged with contempt of court in a wife and child desertion case.

Three days later a deputy arrived from Beaumont to escort Choates back to that town, but he was too late. Choates had died in prison a half-hour earlier. No mention was ever found of an inquest; however, it was said that, at age 29 and the father of two small children, he died of cirrhosis of the liver and complications due to alcoholism.

Dance for Harry Choates. He knew fiddling better than he knew living, and it was the sounds from his fiddle that would last the longest.

Choates' family didn't have the money to bring his body to Port Arthur near Beaumont for burial, so a local radio station raised funds by appealing for contributions. At first his burial plot was marked by only a simple grave marker. Thirty years later some of the Cajun people in the area had raised money for a larger marker dedicated to the "Godfather of Cajun Music." Arhoolie Records, which specializes in folk music, had a more precise epitaph on its album of Choates' recordings, labeling him on the cover as "The fiddle king of Cajun swing."

Much of king Choates' career was spent playing that fiddle at dance halls in the vicinity of Lake Charles, Louisiana. That's the location of McNeese State University, where the fight song is a marching band version of "Jole Blon." On crisp fall football nights the entire student body sways in unison to the music. Nearby is Cajun country where the native music is now more popular than ever. Tour buses pull into the lot outside Mulate's in Breaux Bridge where the dance floor is packed nearly every night. In the town of Eunice, the Liberty Theater has been restored to be the site of the weekly equivalent of The Grand ol' Opry. At spots all along the highways the music is played and the bands' repertoires will include "Jole Blon" just as certainly as "The Saints" is expected of the jazz groups in New Orleans.

When those saints do come marching in, perhaps Harry Chaotes will be in that number, maybe even leading the way with his fiddle. Somehow he seems to deserve a second chance at life. Meanwhile:

Dance for Harry Choates. He knew fiddling better than he knew living, and it was the sounds from his fiddle that would last the longest.

ON THE ROAD

HIGHWAY TO THE EAST

Near the eastern end of Orleans Parish, where the Chef Menteur Highway crosses the Rigolets, stands Fort Pike, a place built by James Monroe for the nation's defense that has more often served the nation as a destination for school and scout field trips. Nothing much ever happened at the fort. Where there has been smoke it has come from the barbecue pits in its shadow rather than from the aftermath of cannon fire. There were episodes when troops were quartered there during the Seminole wars and other soldiers stopped over on their way to Texas during the Mexican War. During the Civil War the Rebels took the fort from the Yankees, but the Yanks got it back. After the war it was left in control of a peace-time force, one lone gunnery sergeant. That sergeant probably represents the fort's history better than do images of a fighting militia. The lone sentinel is indicative of the highway that passes alongside the fort as well. Like the soldier, the Chef Menteur seems lonely — surrounded by history but away from the action.

Generals would buy bigger and more dangerous weapons that made little brick forts obsolete. Another general, Dwight Eisenhower, would become president and sign off on a nationwide interstate system that would make the old federal highways somewhat obsolete as well. Interstate-10 was to the Chef Menteur, which parallels it to the south, what the Strategic Air Command was to places like Fort Pike, a more formidable way of getting the job done.

What is referred to as the Chef is actually part of Highway 90, which begins in downtown New Orleans as Broad Street. Moving towards the east, Broad becomes Gentilly Boulevard and then once it dips for the trestle near People's Avenue, it becomes the Chef Menteur, named after the water channel several miles ahead.

I've never known quite what to think about the Chef, but then I haven't thought about it very much. In earlier days it was the route to the Gulf Coast; billboards along the way told about land deals in places such as Pass Christian Isles. But there was always something faded about its appearance, slightly frazzled. There seemed to be too many suspect spas and run-down motels that advertised special day rates. Its landmarks are few, other than perhaps the sign on the side of Richard's Restaurant, which advertises "Northern Coffee," a snub to a town that takes its rich brew seriously, and the Danziger Bridge, which rises high above the Industrial Canal but not as high as I-10's nearby high-rise.

Few things go as high as the external fuel tanks manufactured at Martin-Marietta's nearby facility, or as low as the city's garbage which is hauled across the Chef to the Recovery I landfill.

Where there is charm, it begins, heading east, after the highway crosses Chef Pass where fishing camps line the road with names such as Manic Manor, Finally Mine, Always Under Construction, Mimi & Gramp's, Corns & Blisters, and Are We Having Fun Yet?

Where there is culture, it is along the intersection of Chef Menteur and Alcee Fortier Boulevard, an area more commonly known as Little Saigon. There the storefronts of two old strip shopping centers now have names that are Vietnamese. This is the commercial center for a group of people who live here because a fortress fell in another part of the world.

Off on the side streets some Vietnamese are living what passes for the American dream in suburban style brick homes, though slightly tattered. The most engaging sight, however, is on the canals where the new locals have moored their boats. It is the water that gives them their link to the old country.

In fact, it is the water that is not only the Chef's reason for being but its salvation. Much of the surrounding area is filled with nothing but unrealized hopes, the industry that hasn't come, the construction boom that never materialized. But the water is consistent, canals and channels linking the gulf with the lake. The water provides for the humble bait shop as well as the grand residential developments such as Venetian Isles where the homes are as rich as the dreams.

That the Chef still provides a setting for dreams somehow gives reason for hope — the Vietnamese kid hoping to make it big in the states; the retiree hoping for nothing more than tranquillity and hungry fish. The fact that a fort is outdated may not be as revealing as the fact that it still stands.

THE VIDEO POKER CORRIDOR

Intuition had taken charge. I had set out to experience video poker, but I wasn't quite sure where to go. There are bars and places that have the machines near where I live, but something told me that would be too easy. It was though the muses of gambling were whispering, wanting to lure me elsewhere. So I followed the message in my mind. "Go," the voices said, "to the Mardi Gras Truck Stop."

My first experience with the machines had been at a lounge called Teal's next to a Holiday Inn in Lafayette. It was the sort of place where a band performed the Drifters' "Under The Boardwalk" in Cajun French and where real drifters and cowboys stood mesmerized in front of the video poker machines.

Draw poker was the main game. For a quarter the machine shows a hand of five cards. Cards can be discarded simply by touching the image of the unwanted card on the screen. Push a button and there are replacement cards. Two pairs or better, you win. It is sort of mindless, sort of simple, sort of addictive. For each winning hand a player gets credits, depending on the value of the hand. At any point a player can push a button that will print out a receipt for the credits won. When I cashed in my receipt the bartender handed over a cool $1.25 which it only took me $6 to earn.

Teal's is not far from an I-10 exit; neither is the Mardi Gras Truck Stop 160 miles to the east. In fact, the Interstate, as it cuts across South Louisiana, may be the video poker corridor of the world. Its exits lead to various truck stops, roadway bars and cafes, each with their bank of machines fronted by players who are always willing to risk one quarter more.

That's what I expected to find at the Mardi Gras Truck Stop, but I was wrong. There was a dining area, a lunch counter, supplies for sale, but no poker machines. Intuition had dealt a bad hand. Not everyone was going bonkers for electronic poker, I thought. But just as I was leaving I noticed an announcement posted on a door. it told about a newly opened place called the Carnival Club, the building located just across the parking lot. Food and drink were available. I stared at the next line of the announcement which added that there were also FIFTY video poker machines. "Fifty!" I thought, "video poker is outgrowing the truck stops." I walked across the lot toward the new corrugated steel building. The facade that covered its top half was colored Mardi Gras purple with gold lettering that spelled out the place's name. This was my first experience with Video Poker architecture.

Inside there was a large bank of poker machines in the center of the room, each fronted by a stool. Other machines lined the walls. On the opposite side was a bar where drinks and sandwiches were sold. To the right was a cashier's window. A cocktail waitress was making a drink delivery. All the employees were dressed in tuxedo shirts and ties — casino style. The cashier's window turned out to be a gambling boutique. Besides servicing the video poker games, tickets for the various lottery games were sold there, too. This being Saturday, activity was brisk for that night's Lotto drawing. If anyone was low on money there was a phone device on one wall into which a person could insert a credit card and, for a fee, order cash. A dollar here, a quarter there, and a person could be a millionaire.

I chose a poker machine next to the one where a little, gray-haired lady was playing. I had hoped to hear some colorful commentary from her as she faced the machine; in fact, she sat silently, staring coldly at the opposition. To up the ante, she pumped a succession of dollar bills into the slot. The machine stared back, maintaining its best poker face.

Video Poker varies slightly, depending on the manufacturer of the machines. Here the machines were made by the Bally Company. Instead of touching the screen to replace a card, one of five buttons corresponding to each of the cards is pushed. Elsewhere, each machine offers options for different versions of draw poker, such as Straight or Deuces Wild. By contrast, each Bally machine plays only one version; however, there are separate machines for each option with a different Louisiana-type name such as "Bayou" or "Cajun." Seasoned players know to pick their machine by name. I picked mine because it was next to an old lady.

Things weren't going so well for her, either. She had broken her silence and seemed to be talking to me. I looked at her and realized that she was really talking to herself, complaining that she had accidentally pushed a wrong button and somehow messed up her wagering. A passing waitress stopped to offer sympathy.

My level of sophistication at playing poker is such that I can report that my best moment was when I drew whatever it's called when all five cards belong to the same suit. For that I won four credits. I could have cashed that in on the spot and gathered $2. Instead I used my fortune as chips to raise the stakes. This was man versus machine. I should have known. The machine had more experience.

After a brief fling, and more luck with a machine that played Deuces Wild, I left. I glanced at the old lady, and she was still eyeballing her machine. It had not been a very profitable venture but it really didn't matter. Intuition had told me to buy a Lotto ticket for that night's drawing, and I was feeling lucky.

THE NEW ORLEANS
OF THE ANTILLES

We were crossing on the ferry. In the distance was the old town the French had founded. Along its narrow streets were buildings notable for their wrought iron balconies. This might have been a description of crossing the Mississippi to New Orleans' French Quarter. It also describes the experience of crossing the bay in Martinique to the Caribbean island's capitol, Fort de France, a town I first became interested in when I read a travel magazine that described it as the New Orleans of the Antilles.

There are some similarities: The streets of downtown Fort de France are like a miniature French Quarter, with traffic equal in proportion. There is a farmers' market where women wearing tignons sell produce including melons and cane. The New Orleans French Market must have looked like that in another era. Much of Fort de France's architecture is similar to the Vieux Carre's, and there are those balconies.

There are some people shared in common, too. New Orleans has the Napoleon House; Martinique has Josephine. Her statue stands in Fort de France's town square. Steamy letters written to her by Napoleon are on display at the sugar plantation home where she grew up. New Orleans and Martinique, two French islands in the tropics, have known both steam and passion.

Then, too, there is Lafcadio Hearn. I first became interested in Hearn not from a magazine but from a parade. In 1989, Hearn's career was the theme of the Rex parade. The diminutive writer lived for a decade in New Orleans. But he also spent time in other places, including Japan and — Martinique. In fact, the best accounts of what life was like on that island in the 19th century were his. Hearn is an important literary figure in Martinique, as he is in New Orleans. But while the island also has a Mardi Gras celebration it has not had the advantage of a Rex parade to tell people about the writer who helped popularize their island. According to a town map, there is a Lafcadio Hearn Square in downtown Fort de France, but that seemed to be known only to the map maker. The square is an unmarked lot, which on a sunny day, and most days are sunny, is filled with vendors from the countryside selling their produce. The various appeals to buy guavas and coconuts are a cackling symphony of French patois. There is no evidence of Hearn being memorialized at that location, but it's the sort of scene he would have written about.

Across the island in the town of St. Pierre, some of Hearn's words do appear. They're in the local museum as part of the text used to describe the pictures of the town having been smothered when Mt. Pelee erupted in 1902. But there is nothing written about Hearn himself. He's just another author whose passages have been borrowed for all time.

Hearn is mentioned, however, at a museum on the outskirts of St. Pierre, though in a supporting role. The museum is dedicated to the artist Paul Gaugin, best known for his paintings of Tahiti but who also got a tropical fix in Martinique. According to the text on the wall, he and Hearn lived on the island at the same time, though it is uncertain if they ever met. The mind wants to insist that they must have. What conversations they might have had! Both were wanderers whose art froze aspects of the island for eternity, though far more poetically than did the lava from Mt. Pelee.

Their topics might have included food. That was one of Hearn's interests. While in New Orleans he even operated a cafe for a short time (until his partner ran away with the money) and compiled a cookbook. He might have found some connection between the local seafood gumbo and the island's fish soup or between the Louisiana version of red boudin and the Martinique native version.

Hearn would have found some differences between the two places as well — many. After all, Martinique is a mountainous island in the Caribbean on which French is the native language and to which people flock to enjoy the beaches. And while New Orleans' own Frenchness has long been diluted by Americanization, the island's people are considered to be French citizens. The bond to the old country remains intact.

Nevertheless, places with wrought iron balconies and Creole cultures share a kinship. At day's end when the ferry returns from the city, the view from the nearby beaches is of the green sea seeming to meet the orange wall caused by the setting sun. The only things cooler than the evening breeze are the rum drinks.

In that setting, the mind begins to wonder: If only New Orleans could be the Fort de France of the Mississippi.

CARNIVAL AT
THE CANNELLTON LOCKS

There was a problem along the Ohio River. The parade had passed, only it passed nearly six hours before the spectators had gotten there.

From down the Ohio River to where it merges with the Mississippi River, then downstream past New Orleans, the commerce of the nation's midsection had been carried by the water. From up the Mississippi and then branching into the Ohio, the traditions of New Orleans have spread, even against the flow. This day a steamboat was going to distribute a load of that tradition along the Indiana shoreline.

Time on a steamboat is in a different realm from what the jet age is used to. Arrival times along the route are spaced generously to allow flexibility for a vehicle that sizzles along at an average speed of eight miles per hour. Even that speed proved too great one morning as word reached the pilot house of the Mississippi Queen that the locals who live near the Cannelton Dam — which is east of Tell City, Indiana, west of Cloverport, Kentucky., and 114 miles below Louisville — had been notified that the people riding the Queen would be throwing beads, doubloons and plastic cups as the boat passed through the dam's locks. The boat, they were told, would be there at 1:30 that afternoon. The problem was that the Queen had already gone through the locks at seven that morning. The captain had to make a decision.

There is no bigger ship on the Ohio's water than the Mississippi Queen, the largest of all the steamboats. So it must have been an impressive sight when somewhere below Cloverport the boat made a wide U-turn, in one instance both comin' and goin'.

Cannellton, In., is a coal-mining town, so the folks there are probably not easily given to frivolity except when there's word of a steamboat bearing gifts passing through. By one o'clock that afternoon, locals were lined along the locks just like people in New Orleans waiting for a parade. And like the New Orleans Carnival, there was royalty, in this case a Queen, in the distance — only it was coming from the wrong direction — a passing monarch doubling back on her tracks, repositioning herself for a grand entry.

So the people of Cannellton, Indiana, and those from Kentucky on the river's other side actually saw two parades. First the Queen went downriver through the locks so it could turn around and head back upriver. Through both passes, the people yelled at the passengers and crew for throws. Here it must be reported that, while Indianians and Kentuckians showed every bit as much enthusiasm as New Orleanians at trying to catch beads and doubloons from a passing vehicle, they have yet to master the language. "Throw me some necklaces," one pleaded. "Throw me some coins," another asked.

As one of those on board, I could have done what was easy and walked to the side deck where the boat, as it passed through the locks, was so close to the people on the side that I could have handed beads to them. Instead, I positioned myself practically at the point of greatest distance, an observation deck on the bow, from which I launched a string of plastic pearls toward a crowd on the Kentucky side. The string never reached the state line, falling with its treasures into the water where, if only there were an oyster, it would seem prolific.

I hadn't realized how much of a tradition our Carnival had become along the lower Ohio until the next evening, when the Mississippi Queen was working itself through another dam's locks 60 miles downriver from Cincinnati. I was standing on the deck when I noticed a man on shore, who was identified by his companion as the mayor of nearby Warsaw, Kentucky, pleading with one of the crew members for plastic cups. Upon receiving his booty, he yelled back that he preferred the Mississippi Queen's offerings over those of its sister, the Delta Queen, which were mostly, "necklaces with yellow things in the center."

When we're having our Mardi Gras in New Orleans — the real Carnival — chances are that alongside those Ohio River towns the water's path will be frozen, stopped by the winter. That's why the people there have to celebrate when the sun shines. It would be nice, however, if on some cold day preceding Ash Wednesday the combination of thawing ice and the churning from a passing tow boat would somehow dislodge a certain string of plastic pearls from below the Cannellton locks and send it to the shore to be found by a passerby. That person might be reminded of steamboats in summer and the Ohio's equivalent of Carnival. But I hope he would know that much further south, near where the big river ends, the water is still flowing and the Carnival is just beginning.

WHERE RIVERS MEET

There's a tradition that says whenever a boat makes the turn at the spot where the Mississippi and the Ohio rivers converge, the thing to do is to throw a penny into the mingling waters for good luck. My luck that day was in being on the Mississippi Queen, the largest steamboat ever, and the biggest craft of any sort to ply the waters of the Mississippi. The Mississippi Queen and its sister the Delta Queen are both domiciled in New Orleans, but they spend much of their time during the summer months working the Midwest streams, which at other times of the year are held captive by ice. On this trip, the Mississippi Queen was heading down the Mississippi from St. Louis, then up the Ohio to Cincinnati. The pivotal turn was at Cairo, Illinois. There seemed to be a thousand coins splashing into the merging waters from the Queen's deck.

When I had last been near Cairo, I descended to it on the train that inspired a song, "The City of New Orleans," as it crossed the Illinois Central's bridge from Kentucky on the way to Chicago. The view from that bridge is one of my favorite in all of railroading. The northbound train usually makes the crossing in the darkest hours of the morning, curving slowly along the trestle. I made a point of sitting on the left side of the coach so I could see both the back and front of the train as it made the curve; but most of all so I could see Cairo below, seemingly dressed at that hour in the urban yellow of its night lights and accented by two rivers.

Now, as the Mississippi Queen glided from the Mississippi to the Ohio, I was seeing Cairo and the bridge from a different perspective. But the real attraction was the water — the mingling of the green and the brown. The Ohio's waters look like green fingers reaching into the Mississippi's mud-brown pelt. The Ohio is a calm, gentle river, tamed by a system of locks and dams. It flows over a bed of fine sand which acts like a prism by turning the water's reflection of the sky's color into a blueish green that happens to match the trees and hills along its banks. The Mississippi, by contrast, takes on the color of the soil and earth it carries, nourishes and redistributes. The mingling of the Mississippi and the Ohio is that of toil with grace.

As the steamboat paddled its way under the bridge, I was able to look up at the train trestle from which I had first come to know Cairo. I was astonished at how small that bridge seemed when seen from beneath. In my mind it had been a towering arch on which trains, like 727's, would begin their descent into the Illinois plains. But from the vantage point of the water, the bridge was just another crossing. It was nowhere near as high as the towering bridges that span the Mississippi in New Orleans, where the river is deeper and thus the passing ships can be bigger and taller. The importance of crossings, however, cannot be measured totally by the height of their bridges. In another era, Cairo, the spot where the waters meet, the northern boundary dividing the Confederacy and the Union, meant an escape from slavery. Not only do waters mingle at that point, but so, too, do the passions of the rural South meet with those of the Midwest. Cairo, located at the southern tip of Illinois, is as close to Jackson, Mississippi as it is to Chicago. The guy whose image is on those pennies that are tossed into the waters, Abe Lincoln, lived on both sides of the river — Kentucky, then Illinois. Like the bridge, he tried to hold both sides together.

These days the juncture, for most, means nothing more dramatic than a landmark in a journey. But dramatic it can be. Rushing to the Mississippi Queen's deck were two women passengers who arrived there too late to see the actual spot of the rivers merging . . . only they didn't know it. They stood at the bow, pointed excitedly and took snapshots of a bend up ahead that they assumed was the rivers' junction. I didn't tell them any differently. Somehow appreciating where rivers meet is not just a matter of geography, but a matter of the mind as well.

COUNTRY RADIO

Scanning the radio dial as I drove through Central Louisiana, most of what I heard seemed to be Rush Limbaugh fading in and out from station to station along the route. He and his callers were pronouncing on the ponderous issues of the day: Bosnia, Whitewater, health care. But then I found the station I was searching for, one on which the news was decidedly different. "I have three kittens looking for a home." one caller announced. "I have 125 square bales of wheat stubble," another voice on the phone said. "Anyone who wants any can give me a call." In the same way that people might feel sentimental about revisiting the ol' small town drugstore they remember as kids. That station for the moment, was where I wanted to be.

Driving from Shreveport, I took a quick roots-like side trip, switching to Louisiana Highway 1 below Alexandria, then heading south through Avoyelles Parish, the place from which many of my ancestors left for the big city. Too many of my visits there as a kid were for funerals. Country radio was there in death as in life. Each evening, the obituaries were announced on radio in French, the native language of many of the people who lived there. Those who knew the deceased would gather to hear the announcement. The death notice in the weekly newspaper would be clipped and saved, but there was extra honor when the obituary was beamed to the country settlements and toward heaven in the language of the bayou.

Marksville and Bunkie are, by Avoyelles standards, the big cities of the parish. The former was best known as the birthplace of Edwin Edwards and is now gaining notoriety as the site of a Tunica tribe casino. Bunkie was named by the man on whose land the railroad developed a town. He chose for the name his young daughter's mispronunciation of her toy monkey. It is a town named after a mistake. Nevertheless, it has had its moments of glory: When John Glenn orbited the earth, one of the television networks reported at one point that the space capsule was over Bunkie, Louisiana. The radio station is KAPB, which is supposed to stand for Know Avoyelles Parish Better. After listening to it for a while I did. I knew, for example, that this was a parish in which there were three homeless kittens. Maybe they could use a bed of wheat stubble.

That information came from the station's midday show, "Swap Shop." Callers in a steady succession announced either what they wanted to get rid of or what they wanted to get. A patient announcer repeated each of the proposed transactions and the appropriate phone numbers. His voice did not sound like the KAPB that I remembered. Announcers in the past spoke in Cajun accents or Southern drawls. This person pronounced in a deep, well-formed, made-for-radio tone. A voice that would have seemed proper announcing the Dow Jones averages dutifully repeated, "a used bedroom set — for sale ."

Most of the advertisers were as I remembered them: a feed store, a dress shop, Roy Motor Company. But there was something notably contemporary about the car dealer's pitch, which announced a casino special. The advertisement urged that people should buy a new car so that they can go gaming in style. There's new money in Avoyelles and it's not chicken feed.

On opposite sides of Highway 1, just south of downtown Marksville, there are two new buildings: one is a WalMart. the other is a casino. A lot of folks were worried about the coming of the WalMart.

Some people were worried about the casino, too. Marksville is the sort of place where the residents don't lock the doors of their homes when they leave; now they're buying new locks. On opening night, the casino's door reportedly had no chance to close. The crowd was overflowing. By 3 a.m. the crowd had thinned to being merely overwhelming.

As I crossed into Pointe Coupee Parish, south of Avoyelles, KAPB's signal was fading. Country places, like country radio, evoke the nostalgia of rural life, yet there is always some current of change. WalMart? A casino special at the auto dealer? Change may be coming at an accelerated pace now. But of greater immediate interest may have been the parting words I heard as KAPB broke into static — someone had a '73 pickup truck, and he was looking to sell it.

TROPICAL BASKETBALL

We hear about the Knicks versus the Rockets or the Bulls versus the Celtics, but since every island can be a world into itself, in one tiny world on the western edge of the Caribbean the big game one night was the match-up of Victoria House versus Tropic Air airline. Victoria House is the classiest resort on the island of Ambergris Caye off the coast of Belize. Its principle owner is a New Orleanian named Mims Wright, who once dodged banditos and bad roads in Mexico to drive a van from Texas to Belize.

Tropic Air is one of two shuttle services that connect the island to Belize City. The twenty minute flight breezes across the green Caribbean with its bright sandspots, descends over the mangrove swamp and touches ground on a long, grassy runway. A universe away are the sprawling, cold, colorless, desensitized airports to the north. At this airfield, when the propellers stop, a big ol' dog might saunter beneath the plane's belly to nap in its shade. Departing passengers are sitting on a white park bench next to the fence.

There's a dirt road alongside the airfield. Victoria House is down the road to the right, the town of San Pedro is up the road to the left. Midway along the street that parallels the shore in town is the church of San Pedro. Next to it is a concrete town square that is the site of an outdoor basketball court. There are some wooden bleachers on either side. This is the hub of sports life in San Pedro, where on breezy summer nights the boys of Ambergris Caye meet to do battle.

There are some differences between tropical basketball and the game that state-siders are used to. One is that the players do not wear high-tech, high-powered shoes with pumps built into the sides. In fact, many of the players don't wear shoes at all: neither do the referees, nor the coaches, nor many of the spectators. In a town where even the mayor does his official business without wearing shoes, footwear, like ties, tends to only be used for special occasions. (One of the spectacles at council meetings is when His Honor stomps out his cigarette with a bare foot.)

Another difference between tropical basketball and the stateside version of roundball is in the level of play. There are no complex offenses, and no slam dunks, since there are no bouncy shoes to launch players towards the goal. The game is simple: run, pass and shoot, while hoping that a tropical gust doesn't blow a long shot off course.

Watching the game is different too. There is a score keeper but no scoreboard. Periodically the score is announced, but it takes concentration to keep track between announcements. The game might be tight, but none of the spectators know it. The team from Victoria House rallied to take the lead, or was Tropic Air still ahead? No one knew for sure, but tension mounted for another reason — the trade winds were pushing clouds beneath the moon. Therein is another difference of tropical basketball — its games, like those of baseball, are sometimes called because of rain.

San Pedro has only one other basketball court, a concrete yard behind the school. But on some days, the goals there are replaced by a tennis net, and on special occasions both are replaced by a tent for a party. There are no golf courses on the island (the attraction here is the sea and a great barrier reef), but if there were, then there'd be no shortage of golf carts, because next to bare feet and bikes the carts are the most common form of transportation. Golf carts, like tropical basketball, are slower and quieter than what Americans are used to, but slow and quiet are why people go to islands. Speed is for the barracuda searching the reef; sound is left to the wind shaking the palms. Victory, on the other hand, is elusive, at least in tropical basketball. The game was suspended by rain.

But on an island of fishermen, wins are more often measured by the number of snappers in the ice chest, and in that there are victories with each boat returning to shore.

There will be no high-rises on Ambergris Caye: there will be no multinational hotels replacing the old buildings of San Pedro. Tourism is where the money is, but the natives are careful about not sacrificing their souls to it. So the caye remains a quiet island where locals stay cool on summer nights by gathering at the town square to watch their boys play tropical basketball. The games will no doubt continue, unhindered by progress, and in that sense, the players have already won the big one.

Fields Of Teams

A Return To The Court

My first memories of City Park's tennis courts are from when I was a kid taking lessons at what seemed to be the hottest part of a summer day. As I think back, there must have been a hundred of us on the court all trying to swing in unison, first a forehand, then a backhand. I think I had one chance to serve a ball which, of course, bounced into the net, and another chance to return a serve, which flew right by me. That was the end of my tennis career up to that point. I discovered baseball that sum-

mer, not only playing it, but watching it in a room where an air conditioner had been stuck into a window. Baseball seemed so much more civil; at least when a person took a swing at the ball and missed there was a catcher squatting behind him waiting to return it. Not in tennis, a game in which too much time was spent gathering balls. In baseball, if a ball was hit over the fence, the person who hit it was applauded. In tennis, for equal heroics the opponent won the point. A few years ago I was at a party where some people were excitedly standing by a television watching Wimbledon. I didn't understand the attraction. Besides, all tennis players look the same.

This year I have returned to the tennis court. There is something therapeutic about going after the ball which becomes a surrogate for workday stress. The key to dealing with stress is not to try to bash the hell out of it, but to wallop it soundly though within bounds.

During my absence there have been some changes in the game. The better rackets are made of graphite, and some have heads wide enough to return a basketball. When tennis players were thirsty they used to go to one of the nearby fountains to get a sip of water; now they carry plastic bottles which contain not water but "fluids." All canvas high-topped footwear used to be known as "tennis shoes." Now there are special shoes for each sport, and the ones used for tennis no longer have high tops, nor are they made of canvas.

There have also been some changes at the City Park courts. My lessons as a kid were on what was known as the concrete courts. In retrospect, I learned more about geography than tennis on those courts. The long cracks in the concrete looked like the paths of the Nile and the Amazon. Those courts were mercifully converted into a parking lot. Now there is a whole set of newer courts, with a surface that looks like it was made from some sort of space age stuff imported from Neptune. But the kids are being deprived. They'll never know what the Nile looks like.

Something else has changed, too — my appreciation for the park. I have lived near City Park all my life, but only now realize its full beauty on those summer evenings when the view to the west from the tennis courts is of palm trees backed by the silhouette of blue streaks against a gold sky. What I have lacked in skill I have matched with awe at the surroundings.

Further evidence that God is a tennis player is the fact that, even when nights are steamy in the rest of the city, there's always a breeze on the tennis courts. The fates, however, do have their impish moments. One night there was a thick swarm of Formosan termites hovering over the court I was playing on. But just as I was about to become part of tennis history by having been in the first match ever to be called because of termites, the swarm suddenly disappeared. If I had been watching myself play that night, I would have left too.

So far I feel like a bit of an outsider in this world of tennis. Many players are beautiful people who look like they have been playing all their lives and who have rackets and shoes probably made from that same Neptune stuff the new courts are made of. One of my best new friends at the City Park courts is the practice wall, a green backstop with a white stripe painted across at the height of a net. I slam forehands, backhands and serves at it, and it always returns the ball. It is always willing to play and never tires.

I have been trying to spend more time on the City Park tennis courts this summer, although here were some distractions, such as watching Wimbledon. Since I have returned to the sport, that grand old tournament has improved and the players no longer all look alike. The real joy, of course, is being on the court where the setting sun and palm trees act as spectators while life's challenges continue: Part of the technique for combating stress involves always keeping an eye on the ball, maintaining a level swing — and being prepared for strange bounces.

WHEN THE SAINTS LAND

I wasn't exactly sure which way to go so I instinctively followed the cars merging onto Airline Highway from the service road that curves in front of the airport. The Saints, I knew, do not arrive at the actual airport terminal but in an area known as "General Aviation" located to the west of the building. It had been a victory Sunday and there would be a crowd to greet the team.

General Aviation is an area of mostly air freight warehouses and hangars. Most of the time the place is void of excitement except for a few times a year when the Saints win one on the road. Then something special happens. A police car barricaded one of the streets, a deputy pointed to the right; he didn't need to ask where I was going. There was only one reason why people, other than those driving 18-wheelers, would be there on a Sunday evening. Somewhere amidst the warehouses a few hundred yelling people were waiting, yet the place is so large that I took several wrong turns before spotting the crowd. To the right, a landing Delta jumbo jet was screeching to its corner of the runway like a running back reaching the end zone. I knew I was heading in the right direction.

West Access Road is the rather unglamorous name for the street where this occasional Fall ritual takes place. Fans were lined along that street up to the point where the landing area was protected by a fence. Police were guarding the gate. In the distance, stairs were being rolled to the side of the plane; a spotlight aimed at it gave the jet a Saintly glow. The jet's door opened and men began descending the steps like gods coming from the mountain, each dressed neatly in a coat and tie.

This is air travel the way it should be. My objection to flying isn't so much being in the air, it's the hassle on the ground: waiting in terminals, standing in lines. It is far different when the pros return from their business trips. From the plane the team members walk a few feet to their cars, which are parked in a secured lot. And if their trip has been successful there are cheering people standing on the side of the road waiting to welcome them home.

All the players drive nice cars, but some of the vehicles have tinted glass as though their occupants are too important to be seen in their private lives. The Saints rolled by, one vehicle at a time. Most smiled at the crowd, a few waved, one excitedly gave a thumbs-up sign. They were living the dream of the American male.

I thought about the day long ago when that dream ended for me — the moment when reality clashed with boyhood. Actually, I hadn't made it very far. It was a Saturday morning practice on a high school football field. The coach had seemed intent on whittling down the squad that day. A bunch of us were picked off one by one, like ducks in a shooting gallery. That afternoon I laid on a sofa at home and watched a college football game on television but felt sad about it; for the first time in my life I knew it wasn't in my future to be on the field. I resolved never to watch football on television again.

Many seasons and TV games later, the glory of winning was being shared communally by all of us along the road who could not experience it personally. People in other towns have several pro teams in different sports to cheer, but New Orleanians have only the Saints. Even among Southern cities such as Houston, Dallas, Atlanta and Miami, the number of home teams to pull for are like the lanes of a four-lane highway on which a traveler can switch from one to another. In New Orleans there is just a single path, and it is lined in black and gold. This is a city that needs to relish whatever victories it can get.

Most of the Saints drove alone; some had been met by their wives or companions. A couple of players were riding on the passenger sides of their respective cars, each holding a baby. Bobby Hebert drove a white Jaguar. Morten Andersen and his companion were in a van. Each team member received an ovation as his vehicle went through the gate. All the players, coaches and administrators seemed polite, though all were reserved — except one. It's hard not to like Tom Benson. The team's owner had opened the sun roof of his chauffeured car so that his upper half could rise through it. He waved and tossed kisses at the Who-Dats along the route. The guy may not know how to block and tackle, but he knows how to genuinely charm people. And his cash registers go *cha-ching*.

It didn't take long for the entire ritual to be enacted. There was little fanfare. Within the span of about fifteen minutes the last of the procession of team members' cars was heading to the highway. The Saints were going home. The fans would do the same.

Rather quickly, the setting became lonely again. It was quiet along West Access Road as I walked back to my car. The stillness was broken only by an 18-wheeler's cab being driven to one of the warehouses. Its sudden appearance was like that of an animal reclaiming its turf after intruders had left the forest. But the forest would be different now. The intruders had conducted a strange victory ritual. In the weeks to come, the mood of an entire community would improve increasingly each time there was occasion for the ritual in the forest to be repeated.

WHERE GOOD FELLOWS MEET

There was an advertisement that once ran in the game program for the old New Orleans Pelicans baseball team. That was in the days when the team played in a stadium located on Tulane Avenue near Carrollton Avenue. The ad advised the fans at the ball park of the following:

> *If the Pels Lose or Win —*
> *Don't Forget the*
> *HOME PLATE INN*
> *Just Across the street*
> *Where good fellows meet*

As it would happen the Pels would eventually lose the biggest game of all, survival, but three decades after the team left the stadium, the advice is still followed. There, among the abandonment of Tulane

Avenue, good fellows and a few gals still meet, eat, drink and some-times talk of baseball.

During many summer days the attention is on the Chicago Cubs, who play in the friendly confines of a television screen. There is probably a natural affinity for the Cubs among old Pelican fans. Like the Chicago team, the Pelicans tended to have losing seasons; and like the Cubs' Wrigley Field, the Pelicans' stadium was an old-fashioned ballpark built in a city neighborhood. It was the sort of place where the kids who lived nearby would gather on game days to earn a few extra dollars.

One of those kids was Clem Lehrmann, who is now the latest in the generation of Lehrmanns to own the Home Plate. His was a family of ballplayers, including two great uncles: Specs and Snooze, who once played for the Pels. Charles "Snooze" Lehrmann was a third baseman, but many years after his playing days I would come to know him in another position — that of neighbor.

It should be the fortune of every boy raised in America to at one point have a former ballplayer living next door. Snooze was driving a taxi by then, but all that mattered was that he once drove in runs. He would also occasionally drive my friend and me to the ball park, treating us to see the Pelicans battle with the likes of the Atlanta

Crackers and the Birmingham Barons. At first my interest was mostly in the hot dogs, which he would also treat us to, but something happened during one of those summer nights while we sat in the stands alongside the third base line. At some magic moment the game being played below was transformed from a curiosity into a passion.

Baseball conquers the heart, I suspect, at the moment when the fan learns enough about the players for the game to become a series of personal dramas: the outfielder trying to break out of a slump, the rookie trying to make the starting line-up, the elder veteran battling both the opposition and time. As I sat there in the stands I was starting to experience new dramas while Snooze and the cigar-puffing old-timers who gathered around him relived theirs from seasons past.

Some of those seasons are remembered through the aged photographs and clippings on the walls at the Home Plate Inn. There are pictures of the old stadium taken in the days when the teams arrived in the neighborhood by train rather than by cable television, back in the days when there was a neighborhood. And there are scenes from earlier days at the Inn when the men of summer gathered for food and drink. Among those in the crowd in one of the pictures is Snooze, not quite the elderly man that I knew, but long after his retirement from third base, no doubt already reliving summer memories.

To the regulars, memories, after all, are what the Home Plate Inn is all about. Those regulars include a former school bus driver. I hadn't been to the INN for several years, but the last time I was there, he was too, sitting, as I recall in the same seat. He's there every Saturday. Phil Johnson, the television editorialist, was raised in the neighborhood, knew the Lehrmanns and goes there for lunch several times a month. There are also some customers who are there more for a poor boy than for the past, but the past's presence is felt, like an umpire watching a pitch.

That the past threw a curve to the Pelicans is a lingering lament. But there is some satisfaction in that there are still good fellows to do the lamenting and a place for it to be done. On the green fields of the imagination the Pels still take the field on summer days, and from the bleacher seats located three decades away, it really doesn't matter whether they won or lost, but that they played the game.

Holidays

FIRE IN THE NIGHT

I'll begin by conceding that I buy fireworks each New Year's Eve. Buying them is perfectly legal. Shooting them, especially within the city of New Orleans where I happen to be each time the New Year arrives, is not so legal. So, for the record, I'll just say that I buy the fireworks for decorative purposes only. I have noticed, however, that the sky over the city is always blinking with light as midnight arrives. Heat lightning, I suspect, even though it is winter. And there is a steady popping noise as though thousands of automobiles being driven from New Year's Eve parties are backfiring at once. (Car engines must get pretty clogged that time of year.) As for all those other people who had been in line at the fireworks stands in Gretna that day, they, too, must have been admiring their purchases — for decorative purposes only.

If, however, shooting fireworks were legal, and if I chose to partake, I would probably have some observations about the ritual, including the following:

- Bottle rockets are my favorite. They're perfect for New Year's Eve because they require empty bottles as a launching pad and those are usually plentiful by that hour. The little rocket comes attached to one end of a slender stick, which is placed in the bottle. Fire touches wick and the rocket is launched, screaming into the night, delivering a warhead that explodes as it reaches its zenith. There's something primal in the experience, man's urge to shoot for the stars, even if the projectile falls short by a few hundred light years.

- Roman candles aren't what they used to be. But then again, neither is Rome. I wonder if the candles are what inspired Jerry Lee Lewis as a kid, because they shoot a succession of balls of fire although too few of them are great. Many of the Roman candles seem to misfire, and even those that do not are often feeble in their propulsion. I still purchase a few, but more out of a sense of tradition than anything else. At best they are a metaphor for New Year's resolutions, high expectations that never quite reach where they are expected to go.

- Black Cat firecrackers pop the loudest. I'm not sure if that's true or not but I was told that as a kid, and there are some things in life that should be accepted on faith and not tested. This is one of them. Incidentally, popping firecrackers one at a time gets boring, and deafening in a hurry. The best way to do it is to ignite the entire pack at once. Just touch the match to the common string that ties together all the wicks, and soon there is rapid fire popping like a miniature machine gun. When it's over there is usually a pile of firecracker paper fragments. There is noise; there is litter. Doing this makes no sense at all, but there is a whole year ahead in which to be proper. Besides, it's all done in the name of science anyway: it's verified for another year, Black Cats do pop the loudest.

- Always buy a few novelty fireworks. Electra, one of the strippers in "Gypsy," had it right when she sang, "You gotta have a gimmick." That's true of fireworks, too. My collection last year included a small cardboard military tank which, if ignited, would have rolled a few feet, stopped and then fired a few rounds of fireballs before self-destructing. Then there was the paper hen which would respond by launching some fiery eggs and then fizzling in its smoke. It's not exactly highbrow entertainment but Electra knew best; every performance needs either a song that can be hummed or a gimmick that can be remembered.

- Always have a big finale. This is basic theater. There must be a big ending. It may cost three or four bucks extra, but the purchase should include at least one bazooka-like gizmo that will launch a canopy of fiery colors into the New Year's sky. Ultimately, it is not the body of a performance that is remembered as much as the way it ends.

And finally a comment on fireworks versus one aspect of the current stage in the evolution of humanity:

- No one carries matches anymore. The same goes for cigarette lighters. Had I actually tried to shoot fireworks last year, I would have discovered that the "punk," a slow burning stick that is supposed to be used to light the fireworks, didn't perform too well. Had I looked for someone with a light I would have realized that, in this age of consciousness about smoking, they didn't have kitchen matches either. The message is clear: If you are going to be shooting fireworks, either bring matches or invite at least one smoker to your party.

It's too bad fireworks are not legal in New Orleans because they fit the city's character so well, combining glitter, celebration and instant gratification. The city's fortunes are like skyrockets, sometimes bursting from the dark with a sudden glow, sometimes veering off course. Yet as each year passes, those of us who care about the city keep looking for a light.

CRASHING THROUGH THE SNOW

I went snow skiing last Christmas, only it wasn't supposed to happen that way. The slope was the bridge that connects Harrison Avenue with City Park. It is a small, routine bridge but on this day, the Friday before Christmas, with the bridge covered with ice, the decline looked like an Olympic ski ramp and my car's tires were giving no more resistance to the snow crystals than a slick pair of greased skis. As the car began its slide it was, for the moment, one of the few vehicles in the city showing momentum, although momentum that was slightly out of control, on a day in which Southern drivers  were gridlocked in Yankee weather. We natives who had always heard about but never experienced white Christmases finally had our chance, and it might have been fun had we been able to ride home from work that day in one-horse open sleighs rather than in cars without snow tires that tended to swerve at every stop. And we might have been cozy had we not lived in homes that were designed for tropical breezes rather than polar blasts. It was a white Christmas all right, and we went crashing through the snow.

Anyone who was in town on December 22nd of last year has tales to tell about the day the snow came. My stories began from the vantage point of a high-rise from which I saw snow for one of the few times in my life and, for the first time, from 18 stories up. From that perspective, the snow did not fall, it attacked. The chilled wind fired the snow clumps at the windows as though a polar machine gun was hidden in the backdrop of the white sky. Snow bullets plopped on the window in a rapid-fire spray.

Below, the freeze was taking siege as people were rushing to get to their homes before it did. We were warned to run the water and to wrap the pipes to prepare for it. The chill came anyway, working its magic in the black of that night, ascending the floorboards, clinching the pipes, turning lawns crunchy white and waxing the streets. By the early hours of the 23rd, Christmas was on ice and so were we. First to go at my house was the hot water. My memories of this white Christmas include preparing to shave by placing a wash rag, dampened with icy water, in the microwave to try to generate some warmth. The floor furnace tried hard, but, like a candle in the blizzard, was overwhelmed.

By Christmas Eve the thaw had begun and the most sought-after man in town was not the one who arrived by sleigh and climbed on the roof but the one who came by truck and crawled beneath the house. For the next few days the true stories of Christmas miracles would be about finding an available plumber.

On Christmas morning I looked under the house to discover nature's presents — two sprays of water coming from pipes that had been pierced by an icy dagger, and a water heater in which the liquid, which had turned to ice, had become so heavy it had broken through the bottom. We speak of Christmases that are merry, but at moments the season seemed to be decked with folly.

There were two shortages in town on the day after Christmas; one was of plumbers, which was just as well because the other shortage was of the supplies needed for plumbing repairs. Yet through it all there were miracles, and mine was finding someone at random from the phone book who agreed to come by just to help turn the rusted water cut-off valve but who stayed around to do the repairs, improvising where needed. And despite the freeze, things Christmasy still happened. People who generally get together still got together, only this time they all had new stories to tell. It had been a rugged holiday but fortunately the grand scheme allowed a second chance a week later when we, in milder weather, could welcome a new year and a new decade. By then the spray from broken pipes had disappeared like reindeer tracks in the snow.

And by now some of the more chilling memories of the immediate Christmas past have melted as well. Once again 'tis the season. And once again from the hallways of old homes designed for Southern comfort, people, perhaps wishfully, will sing of dreaming about a White Christmas.

AN ALL SAINTS' DAY TREK

We were out to honor the saints.

True, some of the names on the epitaphs may not have exactly been saints, but at least we were honoring the custom of visiting the city's cemeteries on All Saints' Day.

Since that day fell on a Sunday last year, I was able to join a small group of people who have made an annual ritual of cemetery hopping.

The idea is to visit some of the city's classic graveyards. The route is set to include stops at the tombs of selected ancestors of those in the entourage. We would gather in front of the departed's tomb where a brief history (sometimes sentimental, occasionally gossipy) would be given. Flowers would be left. The tomb would be tidied. Then we would move on.

Whatever the route is in any given year, the last stop is always Metairie Cemetery where, after the appropriate tomb stops, the group has a picnic alongside one of the ponds. There is an eerie beauty to the place. Like many of those memorialized throughout its grounds, this plot of land has experienced a colorful existence. The main road at the cemetery is an oval, the shape of the racetrack that was once on the site. In 1855 Lecompte, a Louisiana thoroughbred, raced Lexington, a horse from Kentucky, along the oval. It was a celebrated race with high stakes. Lecompte lost, and it was said of the wagering that some plantations changed hands that day. Fate was about to play its hand, too. The racetrack suffered from the Civil War and never recovered. Its obituary was written in 1872 when the track was converted to a cemetery.

As a burial place, new legends would be made. Cars zoom by on the Pontchartrain Expressway which years ago was the path for boats and barges as they made their way along the New Basin Canal. Legend has it that there was a strange red glow on the tomb of Josie Arlington, the famous madam from the city's former red light district. Some thought the glow was mysterious; others said it was just the reflection of a warning light along the canal. History and mystery haunt freely in old cemeteries.

Our first stop this day was St. Roch Cemetery where there was mystery in the small chapel. The chapel generally houses the ex-votos, replicas of body parts, most often arms and legs, left in hopes of a cure for ailments to the affected limbs. The mystery was that the ex-votos were gone, as though the chapel had been robbed of prayer. We later learned that the contents had not been swiped but rather loaned, shipped to the art museum as part of the archdiocese's anniversary exhibit. Sometimes one era's voices become another era's museum pieces.

By the time we reached Metairie Cemetery, and the last of the tombs along the route, we had heard many stories about lives which, were it not for the rituals of All Saints' Day, might never have been remembered. These were not famous people, but they were part of the chain of events by which those of us who were visiting came to exist.

If life presents its mazes, so too does death. Some of the tombs had been easy to find, others were lost in the rows and columns that made up neighborhoods of burial places. One couple in our party seemed to have been separated from us while trying to track down an ancient ancestor. The crisis was compounded because the sandwiches for the picnic were in their car. But somewhere between the marble and the granite those in the group found each other. There would be no lost soul in the cemetery.

A spot near a tree alongside a pond was selected for the picnic. But the gray cloud that was providing shade impishly held back only long enough for the picnic baskets and spreads to be put in place. Then the rain came.

Our ritual was suddenly transferred to a room in my house, where the picnic was spread on a floor. We sat, ate, and, on this Autumn afternoon, truly honored the Saints — who were beating the Tampa Bay Buccaneers.

Somehow an afternoon rain on All Saints' Day is appropriate. The visitors to the cemeteries had come and gone; the neighborhoods of granite and marble were again quiet. Left in the wake were bouquets of flowers, each thirsting for the rain. In this, the unlikeliest of neighborhoods, life in its own way continued.

MOST OF ALL, A GOOD EGG

Among the everyday chickens that were once grown on the small farms of central Louisiana was a small grayish bird with white markings known as the guinea hen. I'm not sure what practical value the guinea had over the other chickens, but every Easter Sunday it did have the rather dubious value of being great for a practical joke.

What made the joke possible was a custom among the area's French speaking people of "knocking" Easter eggs. This was a bit of sport that required some wrist action but, most of all, a good egg. That egg, which would be dyed as all good Easter Eggs should, would be like a weapon in what amounted to a prenatal showdown. As the duel began, the holder of one egg would gently tap the pointed end of his egg against the similar side of the opposition's egg. The tapping continued without mercy until one egg gave in to the stress and bombardment by cracking. At that point the fallen egg would be surrendered to the holder of the conquering egg whose aggressiveness, it might be assumed, required a hard-boiled disposition.

Now among those who were armed with eggs of like lineage there was a certain amount of sportsmanship to this combat — an honest test of perseverance among eggs of equal stature. As sometimes happens in sports, however, there were those who would taint the process. That brings us back to the guinea hen, a bird whose attributes include

producing an egg that is smaller but with a harder shell than that of the average yard chicken. The egg is also a bit darker than the usual variety but when dyed in Easter colors can appear to the unsuspecting as one of the bunch. Were there an office of Commissioner of Egg Knocking, those who use the guinea eggs would be banned from the sport for life, but in the naive world of brightly colored baskets and chocolate candy the occasional bad egg gets by.

Thus would it happen that some kid with a guinea egg as a ringer would wing away those eggs of his competitors. In his conquest he could, as it were, gather all his eggs in one basket.

For most others, egg knocking was a far more genteel tradition practiced for the sport of it and in which winning was not always what it was cracked up to be. For all winners, the problem with victory was that the trophy, after all, was a cracked egg and with more victories came more eggs of similar condition, none of which were suitable for long-term display or barter. There's only one thing to do with a cracked boiled egg and that is to eat it rather soon, a fact that could haunt those whose booty might have been enhanced by the guinea egg con. For a bounty of cracked eggs as prisoners of war, the best hope could be that the week after Easter could be their salad days.

When eaten plain, incidentally, the dyed boiled Easter egg becomes subject to one of the season's great myths. Among egg knockers it was conventional to claim that dyed Easter eggs always tasted better than the conventional sort. This wisdom, passed through generations, was elevated to the status of doctrine, and for good reason, because dyed eggs did in fact have a fuller, richer taste. The reason, however, may have little to do with the magical power of Easter color as much as it did with the fact that usually a day or two passed between the dying and the eating so that the egg was a bit more aged than the everyday plain-clothes type.

Maybe the coloring gave a psychological boost as well, and for those who won their eggs through knocking there could have almost been a bit of the taste of victory. What surprises me, however, is that not more people have had that taste. Since my ancestry is from central Louisiana I grew up assuming that everyone knocked eggs at Easter. But that seems to be yet another endangered custom. In retrospect, the tradition reflects rural life and the farm yard where eggs could be identified with the chicken rather than with the supermarket, and it seems out of place among city folk.

Nevertheless, I have this hankering to see customs remembered. They have a simplicity to them in which the message might be that although life presents occasional hard knocks it is most fulfilling when viewed with the sunny side up.

State Of Grace

The Pope And Me

Never before had I caused so much excitement. There was a line of people on either side of the street. They were yelling excitedly, jumping and cheering. I graciously waved back. Meanwhile my driver pressed on, not wanting us to be late for the even larger crowd that would certainly be waiting at the end of the route.

Maybe it was the Pope, riding in the vehicle behind our press bus, who contributed to the crowd's excitement, but we were willing to capitalize on whatever glory we could get.

It was five years ago this month that Pope John Paul II came to town. For some his coming was spiritual; for some it had an air of celebrity to it, just as if Queen Elizabeth or some other monarch stopped by for a visit; for others it meant nothing at all. For me, it was an adventure.

I had been assigned to be in one of the "press pools" — a group of journalists given access to a specific event who in turn are supposed to share the information they gather with other journalists. My beat that day was the Pope's speech at Xavier University. The pool began, however, at the University of New Orleans' east campus where the Pope said Mass. We of the pool were supposed to meet there to be bussed in unison to the next event. The bus left several moments ahead of the Pope, for whom getting to his limousine amidst a flock of admirers did not come easily. We of the pool faced no such idolatry and were thus able to leave humbly. Once the sirens to our police escort began, however, we became more important.

People along Lakeshore Drive were not accustomed to having the Pope drive by their homes on a Saturday afternoon so they were understandably excited. They had been waiting through a drizzle for a glimpse at the Pope. Suddenly they heard sirens and saw the police escort along the papal path. There was something to see. They knew the Pope wouldn't be riding in the Greyhound bus but they figured we must be important, otherwise why would there be all the commotion? So they excitedly tapped each other on the shoulder and pointed to the bus to draw attention to our passing. Many clapped and cheered, not knowing that we were mere couriers rather than disciples.

In fact, we were a scruffy lot. Many in the group were European journalists worn from following the Pope across his entire American tour. Their muscles bulged from hauling cameras and tripods, their photographers' vests bulged from rolls of film. One French journalist complained that a good cigarette and a place to smoke were getting hard to find in America. They were a fairly cynical group whose mission in life was to find the good photo opportunity and for whom with each passing event on the tour the opportunities began to look the same.

Nevertheless they seemed amused by the excitement we were causing. That excitement continued as the motorcade sped across town to Washington Avenue and then to the Xavier campus. Outside the Xavier wall was a line of well-dressed people that stretched for several blocks. Those in the line were waiting to enter the campus quadrangle to hear the Pope. They too pointed excitedly as our bus whizzed by to the accompaniment of a symphony of sirens. The bus stopped at the main entrance where we were escorted to a large room that had been converted for the occasion into a press headquarters. The efficiency of the organizers was evident. There were rows of tables with telephones specially installed, and there were soft drinks and snacks. We rested while others stood in line. Hardly anyone used the phones, but I did. As I recall, my report went something like this: "So, Mom, we're in this big room at Xavier now waiting for the Pope."

As expected, he was well received by those in the audience who were there to see him as much as hear him. After his talk, the Pope and the people were shown a movie about Catholic education. I watched him watch the movie and thought about the public presence that public

73

people must maintain. With a thousand eyes staring and a hundred cameras ready to click, they can never yawn, rest their eyes for a moment or look disinterested. The papal presence must be maintained. Sometimes with power comes a loss of freedom. I thought about that morning when I had first seen the Pope as his motorcade turned onto Canal Street. What might have been exciting was really sad. Here was this man with a big smile, sitting in the back of a limousine but covered by a box made of bulletproof glass. Did he ever wish that he could again be able to walk public streets whenever he wanted to?

He did rebel a bit when the Xavier activities were over. On the way out, the Pope broke with the format and walked along a barricade shaking hands with the people. He passed the press stand where, to my surprise, among those anxiously reaching out to shake his hand were those scruffy, hard-nosed journalists. The moment was infectious.

After that moment the Pope and the press went different ways: he to his lodging at the bishop's residence and we to the press headquarters at the Hilton. For us, there was no longer a police escort. To those on the streets we were just a bunch of people in a bus. At the hotel I went to the briefing area where, as expected, there was nobody waiting to be briefed, especially since the entire event had been on television and since nothing that would excite the press had happened.

It was quiet on the way home that night. For me the Pope beat was over. But for the others, the next stop was San Antonio, where presumably the Pope, the people and the press would continue the search for those things each was seeking.

MIDNIGHT STAR

Christmas, in a sense, belongs to the evening. The story of the nativity, after all, is sung about in terms of nights that are silent and holy and brightened by a star. And the season's most whimsical myth tells of a jolly little man piloting eight reindeer through the dark to make his deliveries. Easter, with its message of the resurrection, is associated quite properly with the sunburst of a spring Sunday, but for Christmas, the night is as a womb for the dawn that follows.

Maybe that's why the tradition of midnight church services has been so much a part of Christmas, a gathering together as though to be present for the birth. In French Catholic Louisiana some of the most native of traditions flank the midnight mass. Along the river above New Orleans, those bonfires on the levee built to guide Papa Noel on his descent into Cajun Country brunch until it's time to leave for church. In New Orleans, the Creole had a bash after mass in the form of a reveillon, a dinner to end the fast before mass and to begin the pre-dawn revelry.

And if at the reveillion the cups runneth over, so too did the church pews as seen from the preacher's perspective, for this might be the one gathering a year to which the stray sheep would return to mingle amidst the faithful.

An annual gathering of the block is such an event that some Christmases can be dated by them, which brings to mind that this year will mark two years since Father Jack Franko's last midnight mass in New Orleans. During his brief stay here, Franko, who was the administrator of Our Lady of Guadalupe Church on North Rampart Street, became sort of a specialist in midnight masses, perhaps presiding over more of them than most priests do in a lifetime. That was possible because nowhere is it written that midnight mass should be only on Christmas Eve. So he had such a mass every Saturday night and, with the assistance of a local piano player who would round up musicians going to and from gigs, made them jazz masses. At the bewitching hour the old chapel on the edge of the Quarter would rock.

There was a certain funkiness to the masses at the church which was already inherently colorful just because of the nature of the congregation — French Quarter folk, tan Creoles, blacks from the projects, gays, straights, proper uptowners, a few tourists, street people, a nun or two, the deeply devout and an occasional stray journalist. I first went there more out of curiosity, in the same way that a person might check out an act at Tipitina's. And on the best nights what an act it could be, combining jazz, Protestant hymns and the church's rituals. "Amazing Grace," the congregation sang, to the lead of a mellow saxophone.

At its best, the mass could be entertaining, made even more so because Franko had an act of his own — the man could preach, not in the heavy-handed style of an evangelist but in a cool, logical manner tinged with wit. Half past midnight, and no one was dozing during his sermons. There was something spiritual goin' on.

There was some bonding, too. Over time the mass was developing a congregation of its own, a collection of more or less regulars from across the city. There was familiarity to the point that in '87 I even received a Christmas card from Franko. It was made from a photo taken the day the Pope was in town. There was a touch of humor to it, as Franko was one of a line of priests in the background being passed up by the blur of the Pope in the foreground. There was a hurt look on his face, like a school boy being ignored by the teacher.

If only the Pope had had time to look, he might have seen the soulful side of his church. That soulfulness continued to be expressed on midnights before what seemed to be a happy family. But sometimes it's hard to see the fires that are burning in people's minds. One evening there was a message from Franko in the church's bulletin. He had been wrestling with the thought for a long time, his announcement said, and had finally requested a transfer.

His departure came quickly, without fanfare. Had he stayed he could have been a celebrity priest, a big name around town — the star of the midnight jazz mass. Word was, however, that he wanted to work in the missions in Mexico. First stop would be in Texas for a crash course in Spanish.

At first I felt miffed. The best of people can only be divided so many ways, and his congregation needed him too. But then I remembered a conversation I had in high school with a young priest who had just been transferred. There were tears in his eyes as he told of hearing the news of this, the first move of his career. He told of the hardships and dangers of coming into a community, getting close to the people and then being yanked away. He added that that is why older priests sometimes seem distant, because they have learned the pains of becoming attached. We don't fully know why Franko wanted to leave, but the people were clearly becoming close to him. After he left there was an attempt to keep the jazz mass going, but it didn't work — the spirit was gone.

I suspect, though, that there's a renewed spirit in some little village in Mexico. This Christmas Eve the people of that town will gather in their church at midnight. They will sing some native songs and then hear some stirring preaching delivered in newly-honed Spanish. And as they look toward the pulpit they will no doubt appreciate that they are indeed being guided by a yonder star.

LUCY MAKES AN ALTAR

This would be the first St. Joseph's Day altar that Lucy would ever attempt on her own. She remembered as a girl helping her mother and her aunts as they followed their grandmother's commands, making a huge altar that was squeezed into grandmother's living room. The ladies would start baking cookies, so it seemed, almost as soon as the Christmas tree was down. By the middle of March they were stirring tomato sauce, baking cakes and, Lucy's job, stuffing artichokes. She was also in charge of packing the small brown paper bags that were given to all the people who visited the altar. In return for a donation, the contents were always the same: two cookies, a prayer card to St. Joseph and a fava bean, better known as the Sicilian lucky bean.

Lucy could use a bushel of luck at this point because things were not going well with her altar making. Grandma, she recalled, had made her altar each year because she had claimed to have seen St. Joseph in a vision and he had instructed her to do so. The other old ladies who made the altars she had visited as a kid did so for various reasons, but usually to thank St. Joseph for having granted a favor, most often, it seemed, one having to do with helping a family member who was sick. But the malady that the saint was best known for curing was malnutrition. As the legend went, he became the patron saint of Sicily for having rescued the islanders, who had prayed to him for relief, from a famine. For that feat, food altars have been built in his honor ever since — altars of such richness that it might be said Joseph delivered his people from starvation to indigestion.

Lucy's altar, she feared, wouldn't be one to make Joseph's all-time Top Ten List. She had made her promise to Joseph a year earlier for no good reason other than she thought it would be fun. She was wrong. Lucy had not considered that she would not have a platoon of family members at her command as her grandmother had. The next generation was scattered all over with even the older kids off in an apartment on their own. The family circle had gotten flat. Then, too, grandmother had never had a job, other than taking care of her house. Lucy, on the other hand, had a clock to punch. When she had made the promise to St. Joseph last year she had a decent clerical job with Amoco. But when the company closed its regional office, she was left behind. Her new, lower wages at the supermarket could pay for dinner but not for a feast. In the past, Lucy would have prayed to Joseph for help. But since the altar was being built to him that seemed sort of like begging from Peter to pay Peter. This scrape would have to be faced without heavenly intercession.

Fortunately there would be intercession from Rosemary, Lucy's friend, who had a car and agreed to help. Once Lucy determined that she could squeeze out $50 for the project, they went to Brocato's to buy some Italian cookies, then to Central Grocery in the Quarter for some anise — a must seasoning — and some olive salad. From the grocery store where she worked she bought a whole drum fish and some artichokes. They even added to the collection a cabbage that Rosemary had caught in the St. Patrick's Day parade. Lucy wondered if the two saints, Joseph and Patrick, had ever crossed paths on earth in the same way that the local parades of the Irish and the Italians do. But Rosemary reminded her that Patrick was one of those saints that Pope Paul said might not have been real. The Irish believed in him, but as her grandmother used to say, what do the Irish know?

They know enough to have a good time and not to make altars, Lucy thought, as she stayed up late that night baking and preparing. She was most adept at stuffing the artichokes and filling the paper bags. By the next morning, however, she was able to arrange the food on a card table she had unfolded in her front room. Her fish looked soggy and the cake she made, which was supposed to look like a lamb, looked more like a gerbil, but the cookies from Brocato's seemed just fine. In her pantry she happened to find an old St. Joseph votive candle set in a glass vase that was chipped at the rim. It seemed like it would be a sacrilege to throw it away, so she lit it but placed it out of sight on the top of the bookcase in the front room. All that was missing now was the dried palm leaf she had saved from last Palm Sunday. That she attached outside near the front door, the traditional sign that there was an altar which was now open to visitors.

As it happened, visitors were few because Lucy had forgotten to put a classified ad in the *Times-Picayune* under the altar listing. Among those who did see the homely little altar was the mailman who Lucy coaxed inside. He was very polite in speaking of the altar's beauty and even left, in the empty goldfish bowl, a dollar for the poor.

Next were some kids who were selling tickets to a church raffle. They were confused about the altar and wondered if there were any Oreos on it rather than fig cookies. They left after Lucy bought a ticket with the dollar in the bowl.

Then she heard a crashing sound behind her. The card table had collapsed, with the fixings of the altar tumbling on top of it. The lamb that looked like a gerbil was decapitated, specks of its white icing were now on the fish and there was artichoke stuffing on the fig cookies which were dangerously near the broken pieces of glass that had been the fish bowl. Lucy stared, took the palm down from the front door, and then cried a little.

Rosemary took Lucy to the movies that afternoon to help her get her mind off the disaster. The friend wondered if Lucy would ever build an altar again; Lucy wondered the same. Neither had noticed that when Lucy straightened the room that she had overlooked one item. The votive candle to St. Joseph on the bookcase — the one with the cracked rim. Its flame was tiny but was somehow now glowing brighter than ever.

New Orleans A La Carte

Steak And Politics

Someone at my table suggested to the waitress that the restaurant should have revolving aisles to make it easier for everyone to see who is at which table. At most steak houses people want just the opposite. Indeed, a few blocks away at Crescent City Steak House, there is such a tradition of steak and anonymity that there are drapes fronting the booths. But at Ruth's Chris on Broad Street, on certain days, the purpose is either to be seen or to see who is being seen with whom.

Those certain days are the ones that have some sort of political significance, most recently the last day of qualifying for this fall's elections. In the kitchen the cooks have pride in steaks; in the restaurant, politicians stake their pride. Styles differ — even among opponents for the same office. One candidate for congress was making the rounds shaking every available hand. Nearby, one of his opponents sat shyly while huddling with his campaign staff. All around, politicians, and politician watchers, watched.

And if they weren't watching they were whispering. In fact, part of the sport is to watch who is whispering to whom, and to wonder about what is being whispered. Politicians, the successful ones, are fine whisperers, who know how to modulate their voices while keeping a watch on the rest of the room — partially to watch others, but also to keep an eye on who is watching them. Power, after all, can be measured by the number of people who are wondering about, or — better yet — made nervous by, what a particular individual is whispering. The steaks may sizzle, but so might the rumors.

There are stories to be told as well. One person lamented that qualifying day isn't what it used to be. He remembered the days when former State Senator Nat Kiefer would be prepared to run candidates for whatever offices were strategically necessary. "We'd all be carrying a couple of qualifying forms," he said with a laugh, "and Nat would have more strategies about who to put in which race than an NFL playbook. It's just not the same anymore."

Still the same, however, is Ruth's Chris as a political hangout. Why it became a hangout is one of those mysteries sort of like why the purple martins chose the Causeway as a place to roost during the summer. Unlike the martins, however, the location probably has nothing to do with the setting sun. In fact, when the restaurant expanded several years ago, it became windowless. That's no loss though, because politicians are birds to whom the changing season are marked by election calendars rather than solar cycles. The real reason may have something to do with the place being on Broad Street and thus a straight shot from the courthouse. There may also be something about the mood of the place.

Ruth's Chris, like Crescent City Steak House, originally flourished in the area primarily because of its proximity to the racetrack. It was the sort of hangout to which horseplayers would go after a good day. There are common bonds between railbirds and politicians, all of whom are astute observers of the race and know the advantage of picking the right horse.

They also know the benefits of having the proper vantage point. For those whose purpose is to be seen, a table in the middle is, of course, the best. But for those who are there for the business of seeing, a corner is the best location, and that is where a local pollster and a former legislator were located as they surveyed the action. Politicians love corners because they are great for both whispering and viewing, without having to worry about who is behind or on the sides. In fact, the political extension of the American dream might not be a chicken in every pot as much as a steak in every corner.

There was also some verbal cornering going on: One judge taunted a state senator, announcing that he was going to send him a drink. Only, the judge added good-naturedly, the drink would be delivered in increments of one-third at a time, "the same way you gave us a pay raise." The senator never received that drink but it really didn't matter. He was there for the political spectacle, and for that, his cup was running over.

THE HOMETOWN PIE

There are two empty package wrappers next to me now. Each, until a few moments ago, contained a Hubig's pie; one is the pillow-shaped type pie — the style coated with glazed sugar. And the other is the typical round, pie-shaped pie. That the wrappers are now empty is due to journalistic research, the pursuit of the truth that this profession calls for — and the truth is that I like Hubig's pies. Not that I hadn't known the verdict before the research.

Hubig's pies seem to have always been around. Made in New Orleans, they are the ultimate neighborhood store-bought lunchtime dessert. I grew up knowing of the pies as the chaser for the ultimate New Orleans store-bought sandwich, Mrs. Drake's. In fact, the classic Mrs. Drake's luncheon meat with pickle sandwich, followed by a Hubig's sugar-coated apple pie, has fueled many work days in this city. All that's missing from the combination is Big Shot Cola, which, when it was bottled in New Orleans, rounded off the triumvirate of locally made lunch stuff. Each was even personified by their own characters as logos. For Big Shot it was a drawing of a guy with a tattered top hat who was smoking a cigar. On the label of Mrs. Drake's sandwiches is a yellow duck, presumably Drake herself, wearing a chef's hat. And Hubig's pies are represented by a caricature of a corpulent chef holding a pie in his left hand and with the name "Savory Simon" across his cap. An ancient television jingle ricochets from the mind in which the voices are singing of "Savory Simon the Hubig's pie man."

Before the Big Shot trademark was sold to an Arkansas bottler, the local manager explained to me that the appeal of his product, which came in big bottles and tended to have heavy, sweet flavors such as pineapple, was to laborers who needed something to go with a hefty but inexpensive lunch. That may be part of the pies' appeal as well, although in the age of yogurt that appeal may be endangered except to people such as myself who appreciate Hubig's just for being a local business. In fact, the location of the Hubig's factory on Dauphine Street in Bywater typifies both its market and my affection. It is not in a suburban industrial park but in an old riverfront neighborhood, the sort of place where longshoremen would have once gone to a neighborhood store owned by German immigrants to get lunch. The pies, like the neighborhoods, are things of nostalgia.

But while the neighborhoods have changed, the pies have not. A Hubig's pie today tastes just like it did the very first time I had one back in grade school. The packaging looks exactly the same, too, although there have been a couple of concessions to crafty modern marketing. For the glazed pie, someone figured that the product could suddenly be made modern by adding the message, "Microwave 25 seconds for a delicious treat!" And as a concession to the pizza vendors of the world, the regular pie, which is the same size as ever, is now described on the package as being "Deep Dish." Other than those changes, and the inevitable price increases (although 60 cents is a bargain), this is still the same pie that guys on the docks once ate between banana boats and that I had during recess. And ol' Savory Simon hasn't aged a bit.

There is another pie, eaten in the same culinary circles as Hubig's, that isn't made in New Orleans but should be — because somehow it seems to fit the city's personality — and that is the classic Moon Pie. Some impish maskers have been known to toss Moon Pies from floats in Carnival parades, and I have a personal tradition — actually I've just done it once but I intend for it to become a tradition — of watching the television meeting of Rex and Comus that closes the Carnival season while toasting the occasion with a Moon Pie and a glass of champagne. A company in Chattanooga makes the pies, which are really marshmallow sandwiches and not real fruit pies like Hubig's, but the products now have something in common. Printed on Moon Pie labels these days are instructions for microwaving them. (For those to whom every second counts, the recommended time for a Hubig's is 25 seconds while for a Moon Pie it is a quicker 20 seconds. But since both have always been eaten right out of the wrapper, why bother?)

Those considerations aside, the Hubig's gets high marks in my mind, not only for nostalgia and taste but, on the basis of pure parochialism, just for being a surviving local business in an age of international conglomerates. There aren't many rules that I live by, but one of them is that when it comes to pastries, the hometown pie always takes the cake.

LUNCH AT ROCKY AND CARLO'S

There are some who might think that Rocky and Carlo's restaurant and bar may not be the ritziest of places, but the sign inside should dispel that impression. "No Shoes. No Shirt. No Service" it says. In a way, Rocky and Carlo's is sort of like Antoine's: It has its dress standards, too. But just because it demands a shirt and shoes of its customers does not mean that the place isn't tolerant of all people, as another sign, this one out front, assures: "Ladies Invited."

On any day, many of the ladies and gentlemen of Chalmette and vicinity pack the place, located on St. Bernard Highway in the parish of the same name. And while the folks at Antoine's can brag about being located in the Vieux Carre, the staff of Rocky and Carlo's can boast that they are located just across the highway from the Mobil refinery.

It is a setting that influences the menu. This is hearty food, the sustenance of laborers and their ladies, who form a line in front of the counter behind which the workers hurry huge pans full of the day's offerings to those doing the serving. The stellar item on Rocky and Carlo's menu has always been the macaroni and cheese, a rich pasta treatment appropriate as a side dish with anything, and the choices are many. I had the fried chicken along with the macaroni and an order of what is still referred to as "wop salad" (with no offense taken by the Italians who run the place). The prices are cheap and the servings are large enough to feed nearby Plaquemines Parish. In fact, the servings are so large they create a secondary business for styrofoam cartons, which are sold at the cash register for 25 cents apiece. We had so much leftover food that we needed two of them.

That cash register just may be the focal point of St. Bernard Parish life, in front of which it can be counted that most everyone who lives in or visits the parish will pass sooner or later. It is both a pay station and a community billboard where one day, alongside the cashier, a stack of leaflets announced the grand opening of Bee's Hair Salon located on Lafitte Court in Chalmette, "Next to Pancho's."

Pancho himself might be one of those standing in line for macaroni and cheese; he plus the usual collection of refinery workers and, one Friday during lunch, soldiers dressed in camouflage fatigues. Also in line were office couriers on a mission to pick up shopping bags full of poor-boys-to-go.

In fact, there were so many poor-boys being ordered that a crisis was mounting. As the workers hurriedly assembled the sandwiches, each noted the depleting supply of french bread loaves. Over and over the fear was repeated, "We're running out of french bread!" The warning was issued so often that one sandwich maker asked caustically, "Is there an echo in here?" That echo might have continued had it not been for another sound, that of a vendor entering the kitchen. The bread man had arrived. Lunch would be saved because of a warrior carrying loaves.

Those loaves would be multiplied into poor-boys, the day's fuel for the parish's work force. Fuel which, like that being produced at the refinery across the street, is in a supply greater than what is needed to satiate the demand. "Those poor-boys are so big," a truck driver told me later that afternoon, "that I go and order half of one. A lot of places don't do that, but you have to at Rocky and Carlo's." The truck driver was sitting behind the counter of a trailer converted into a barroom located on the far end of Delacroix Island, the spot that is way down on the far water's end of St. Bernard Parish. It is so remote that a sign at the dock even proclaims the place to be the "End of the Earth." But when a place is legendary, the legend follows even to the ends of the earth.

And if the customers are content it is because of the quantity and quality of the food and not the decor, the style of which might be described as being "Basic American Truck Stop" — though not quite as glamorous. The charm is in the people, who include corpulent housewives, refinery workers with long hair hanging from beneath their hardhats and the kitchen help, some speaking off-the-boat Italian. A few of the customers are leaning against the counter but most are at the tables, where the experience of the rich colors comes not from the interior design but from the macaroni and cheese. Ceiling fans spin quietly, sending a slight breeze onto diners who may be staring at orders of stuffed peppers, fries and macaroni. The mathematics of dining is different along the St. Bernard Highway, for in that world half a plate is still equal to a full plate anywhere else.

THE FIG AT THE TOP

For the rest of the nation July is the month to celebrate the country's revolution, but for Newt that month has been the time for his own personal revolution as well. It is when the primal spirit within him revolts, for a morning at least, against the staid person he has become.

Thus it is now a ritual that on a Saturday morning in July he gets the ladder from his carport, ties it to the top of his automobile, and then heads to the city to what was his grandmother's old house on South Genois Street. As landlord of the property where he spent so much time as a kid, Newt has always made sure that each new set of tenants understands that he has full access to the backyard and particularly to the magnificent old fig tree that his grandfather planted and from which Newt plucked so much fruit as a kid. In those days he did so while scaling the branches to dizzying heights never reached by the spaceman within his imagination.

Many years later Newt was still trying to reach those heights in defiance of fate, which kept increasing the odds so that each year as the tree got a bit taller the roof of the adjacent shed, which acted as his launching pad, became a little less sturdy. Nevertheless, this was the annual event with which Newt measured both the passing of time and

his ability to deal with it. The most daring feat in his life these days was his yearly attempt to grab for the fig at the top of the tree. He and the tree had grown together and, as Newt saw it, there would continue to be hope for both as long as each could still be reaching toward the sky.

This year Newt was aided by his tenants, a guy and a girl with a fascination for electric guitars which, so the neighbors complained, were occasionally played too loudly, too late at night. Besides that they seemed okay, although they, like all who had lived there since Grandmother had died, had never paid much attention to the riches growing in the back; to them, picking figs was something old people used to do. That is, until last year when Newt, looking for someone with whom to share the bounty, had the wisdom to remind the couple that the fruit from this unattended tree was, after all, organically grown. Their interest was piqued as they began to think of the tiny bulbs as a natural earth food. So this year they were here to help, picking from the low branches while Newt, turning down their offers to take his place, climbed the fragile limbs to the top.

Ascending a fig tree, after all, is an act best left to the veterans. Newt stepped from the shed roof to the top of the ladder, which had been positioned through a maze of twigs and then onto some of the bigger branches near the trunk. From there he began his slow climb, stopping to pick a fig here and there, gently dropping his tender captives into the basket on the top of the ladder. Like any voyager he encountered the mysterious along the way, such as the milky, white, sticky sap that gets on the hands — and the hazards, such as the occasional branch giving way to his body weight. But like a seasoned mountain climber who knows the sturdy ledges and rocks, Newt perched on what he knew to be the tree's more reliable arms which, in turn, seemed to use their muscle to support him as he eyed a fig at the top. It was a large bulb, maybe twice as large as the rest, so purple that it seemed to be bursting with sweetness. Its position, however, atop the highest branch presented a formidable challenge as Newt reached, strained, reached some more and shimmied up the trunk as far as it would allow — traveling into space further than any had gone — stretching all he could to softly grab the fig and break it from its twig. The branch swayed with his weight, creating such a jolt that he dropped the fruit which plunged to earth and was fielded by the tenant, who re-activated his long-dormant baseball skills in making a graceful catch.

Meanwhile the swaying branch took Newt in the direction of the shed where his waving legs made contact, like the landing pods of a space capsule, with the shed's roof.

Moments later Newt arrived back on earth to the jubilation of his ground crew. The fig from the top was like his moon rock, something from above to be prized although a close examination revealed that it had been pecked mercilessly by alien birds. But in this moment of conquest Newt sensed what all great adventurers surely must feel: the thrill of triumph is not so much from the trophy as from the adventure.

THINGS PAST

GONDOLA CONFESSIONS

I really, really wanted to ride the gondola.

Ten years ago, that ride first appeared along the riverfront. It was located at the water's edge of the World's Fair and was supposed to be one of the event's main attractions. There was a tower on the East Bank and another across the river on the West Bank. The towers supported a moving cable from which little capsules clung while carrying their passengers across the nation's spine.

From the beginning, I couldn't think of anything I would rather do than to be locked in a glass cage dangling on a cable over a deep, raging river. I really, really wanted to ride that thing.

My first opportunity would have been on the day before the Fair opened — media day, the time for showing off the site to the press. But things weren't quite ready by that day. Workmen were busy. So as much as I really wanted to ride the gondola, I thought I shouldn't rush it. I might have gotten in the way of a welder or someone; besides, maybe the paint wasn't dry.

My next opportunity came the next day. I really, really wanted to get on the gondola, but the opening day crowd was big and the lines were long. I thought it would be better to wait. After all, it was only May and the Fair would be open until November. There would be plenty of opportunities ahead.

In fact, there were many days during the Fair's season when the crowds were not big and the lines were not long. I still really, really wanted to ride the gondola, although other, less courageous people might have been bothered by such trifles as my memory of the day when the gondola was stuck. I was walking along the grounds when I looked up and saw some guy suspended in a bubble. The capsule he was in had just crossed under the East Bank tower and was beginning its descent when the cable stopped moving. There he was, dangling over the Fair encased in a plastic shell on a hot, humid day. That seemed like fun. I wished it had been me in there.

Nor was I bothered after watching the mechanism of the gondola system at the point where a departing capsule clutched onto the cable. The hold seemed tenuous. But why worry about the gondola crashing into the Mississippi? Just think what a picturesque splash it would have made.

I wasn't concerned either about an account from a friend who took his kid out on the gondola. The kid screamed all the way. After all, he was just a kid and I'm a man.

As much as I really, really wanted to ride the gondola, the reason why I kept delaying the ride had nothing to do with fright. I was just trying to be polite. After all, many of the Fair's patrons were from out of town and they wouldn't have the chance to come back. They should have had the first opportunity on the gondola. We locals could hang from a cable anytime we wanted.

By closing day of the Fair I still hadn't been on the gondola. But, as much as I really, really wanted to ride it, it just didn't seem right to take the space of those who, by that day, may have had a sentimental attachment to the ride. Besides, it had already been announced that the gondola would remain in operation after the Fair closed, so there would still be a lifetime of opportunities to take the ride. I was so glad.

Of course, once the Fair closed there weren't as many reasons to be at the site. And there was a new concern. It had been suggested that the gondola could be used by commuters from the West Bank. So as much as I really, really wanted to ride the gondola, it worried me that I might take the seat of someone rushing home to the arms of a waiting family. What if that person was bringing ice cream to the kids? During the time that person spent waiting for the next capsule, instead of being in the one I had taken, the ice cream might have melted. I didn't want to be responsible for the disappointment.

Then one day the announcement came: The gondola was being shut down. What a blow. Eventually the capsules were sold. By this year, a decade later, the towers were removed. Someone told me they saw a capsule sitting on a lawn along Bayou Lafourche near Golden Meadow. That seemed like a capsule I wouldn't mind being in. Besides, if I craned my neck a bit, stared across the road and squinted my eyes just right, Bayou Lafourche could look something like the Mississippi. Sitting in that capsule parked on someone's lawn might be something like being in the gondola when it was stuck — just like in the good ol' days.

Now there is no sign of the gondola that once was along the riverfront. All that's left are the memories I might have had. I really, really wanted to ride it. If only I had had the opportunity.

PONTCHARTRAIN BEACH: A DECADE LATER

Amusement parks, like Christmases, are the sort of thing that are most often spoken about with nostalgia. For New Orleanians, nostalgia is all that's left when the subject is Pontchartrain Beach, a place along the lake where the Ferris Wheel could be the coolest place in town on muggy summer nights, and where the salt-scented lake breeze could hit like a fist as the Big Zephyr, the park's antique roller-coaster, made its downward plunge. Now even the most recent memories are becoming misty nostalgia. It is hard to believe, but after this summer it will have been a decade since Pontchartrain Beach closed for good.

When "the Beach," as it was commonly called, ceased operation there was talk about a residential development going up on its site. That never happened. The space has defied the future, remaining unoccupied, as though it is a sacred burial ground of summers past. There are only a few ruins of the old amusement park left. It is a ghost town where ghost screams from the Zephyr, racing along the track, or from the Wild Maus, seemingly about to leap into the skyline, haunt freely.

Memories have layers. There was nothing special about the burgers served at the Beach during its waning years, but what I remember is the fragrance of burgers when I was a kid. The smell of the midway was that of onions frying. I had never seen mustard jars as big as the ones from which we splashed the burger.

When I was a kid . . . Goodness! Flag Days at the beach. A zillion boy scouts, and I was one of them, walked along the midway in a procession to honor Old Glory and, perhaps more importantly, to take advantage of the free rides offered to us for our efforts. Here, beneath the shadow of the waving flag, was the law of supply and demand at its worst. Because there were so many of us demanding a ride, the lines were long. Because the lines were long the number of revolutions per ride was shortened. But that didn't matter. We were, after all, men in uniform, somehow fulfilling our patriotic duty by riding The Bug.

There are two famous sons of Beaver Falls, Pennsylvania; one is Joe Namath, the other is The Bug, the Beach's oldest ride, which was manufactured in that town. I will confess now that I was really a closet ride phobic. I never rode the Ragin' Cajun, which turned its riders over while performing a corkscrew loop. I appreciated conceptually but barely tolerated the Zephyr. And one time was enough on the Wild Maus. But The Bug was the ultimate thrill ride for the timid. Riders in each unit of this mild roller coaster sat around a metal wheel which they clung to while being jostled and bounced just enough to provide the thrills but not so much as to prompt visions of their lives passing before them.

To me, daredevilry was to be watched and not experienced, and most of that watching was directed towards the big stage where there were acts twice a night. Was riding up front in the Zephyr any less daring than the person in the spotlight who was diving from a tower into a vat below?

As kids we never fully understood the implication, although it did seem wrong, that blacks had to go to a separate amusement park several miles away in a more desolate part of the lakefront. By the time the Beach was integrated there was a force at work which ultimately closed the park. Tastes were changing. People had gotten used to theme parks such as DisneyWorld and Six Flags. Besides, the year was 1983. Next year there would be a world's fair in New Orleans, and all the attention would be on the other side of town. An old-timer explained to me that in the old days amusement parks were built on the outskirts of town where the land was cheap; now the towns were catching up with the outskirts. The land where the Beach was located was becoming too valuable. Certainly, or so it seemed at the time, with the post-fair boom there could be better use for the site. All those things considered, in the end, Pontchartrain Beach just wore out.

During its later years, there was a fancy restaurant at the Beach called the Bali Hai. It was a feel-good sort of place that cashed in on the Polynesian enchantment created by the movie, "South Pacific." The interior was decorated with bamboo. Polynesian music was played in the background. It was a place for special occasions, and whoever the special occasion was for sat in a huge, fan-backed rattan chair. A Tiki Bowl, the house specialty drink, was made with rum, served with two straws and garnished with a paper umbrella. Bali Hai tried to evoke the mystery of the South Seas and whatever places were in the distance. Its mood overshadowed the fact that we were merely on the South Shore, with only Mandeville on the other side.

Amusement parks were never about fact, but rather fantasy. For a brief spin we could be where our minds wanted us to be. Until the ride came to an end.

SICILIAN DAYS

I didn't realize it then, but I was experiencing the last days of the French Quarter as an Italian neighborhood. I think about those days anytime I am in the Quarter along blocks in the vicinity of the French Market, especially during March when St. Joseph's Day reminds me of the richness of ethnic traditions that are too often lost by assimilation.

If the neighborhood had a heart it was the church in the 1100 block of Chartres Street known as St. Mary's Italian. To a neighborhood of immigrants it was the key to survival, not only in heaven but, more immediately, on earth. I came to know that neighborhood from visiting my relatives who lived there, none of whom were Italian but all of whom were like immigrants, having migrated from the rural poverty

of French-speaking rural Louisiana. As was true of their Sicilian neighbors, they had moved to the city looking for work, and a foreign language was their primary tongue. My relatives were, in effect, a sub-minority living amidst a larger minority forging its own culture in those neighborhoods where prior history had been claimed by the Spanish and the urban French Creoles.

To this day there are still blue tiles spelling out the names of long-gone Quarter entrepreneurs at the entrances of some storefronts. And the produce markets still have Italian names. Central Grocery on Decatur Street imported olive oil, beans and dried fish from Sicily as well as meats and cheeses. At a nearby ice cream shop and bakery, the three sons of an immigrant named Angelo Brocato provided carhop service for those who craved their father's spumoni or, if it was summer, lemon-flavored ice. Brocato's pastries redefined Italian baking.

One of those Brocato sons was also named Angelo, and many decades later I listened to him recall those days at the shop. Each morning one of the kids of an Italian restauranteur named Diamond Jim Moran would come in carrying an empty pitcher which was to be filled with lemon ice. Back home the ice would be spread on warm Italian bread as breakfast.

It was dinnertime, though, that made Moran famous. He operated a fancy restaurant in the Quarter, made fancier by the legend that he would sometimes plant a diamond inside one of the meatballs being served. I remember once, for some special occasion, eating there as a kid with my parents and seeing Diamond Jim himself, a big man with rings and a tie clip that sparkled with diamonds. In what was like high-stakes king cake eating, I ordered meatballs and spaghetti hoping to find a foreign object hidden in my food. I left that night richer only by having met Diamond Jim.

Moran was not the most important person in the neighborhood, though; from my perspective, that title went to a priest, Father Vincent Liberto, the pastor at St. Mary's Italian. He was a combination celebrity, social leader and confessor. Probably any Italian family in New Orleans today was touched at some point by Liberto, who did most of the marrying, burying and baptizing for the community. Across the street from the church was St. Mary's Italian gymnasium where Liberto ran a boxing program for the tough Quarter street kids. From its ring came contenders and champs such as Willie Pastrano, who won a world title. The gym was also the neighborhood's social center; I remember going to a reception for one of my older cousins who had just gotten married across the street. This was a place for matches, those made by boxing promoters and those made in heaven.

Today, there is little in the neighborhood that recalls the Sicilian days. Angelo Brocato's original store moved to Mid-City. The buildings where my relatives formerly lived are now richly restored hotels, guest houses and homes. Montalbano's Grocery in the Quarter once had a year-round altar to St. Joseph. The grocery has been long closed, and not even on St. Joseph's Day have there been any altars in the neighborhood lately.

No one can say exactly when the Quarter's Italian days came to an end. I remember one St. Joseph's Day in the early '80s visiting an altar across the street from the Quarter in Marigny at the home of a Mrs. Vincent Piccatacci. The food altar glittered from the front room of a little shotgun house, just as was once common in homes throughout the neighborhood. That's all gone, though.

There are those who lament that the Quarter is not what it used to be. To that I answer that it never has been what it used to be. It is a living neighborhood that, even within the preservation guidelines for its buildings, is constantly changing. Today's experience is tomorrow's nostalgia. Nevertheless, I suspect that tomorrow will be hard put to capture the imagery of the Sicilian days. Life goes on, but for the sake of the city, wouldn't it be grand to one morning in the Quarter smell the aroma of warmed Italian bread and see a kid hurriedly returning home from the store with his pitcher full?

THE LAST DAYS

A college student approached Miss Viola, who was on the other side of the counter, and announced loudly enough for everyone in the drugstore to hear, "Viola, we wanted to give you a present, but we weren't sure what, so we decided to give you this." Viola smiled faintly at her "present," a trio of horn players who began a few bars that would segue into "St. James Infirmary." Perhaps a funeral dirge would have been even more appropriate as the crowd gathered along the counter for the last Friday of Viola's gumbo and the beginning of the last week of operation for Schweikhardt Drugstore.

There have been many, too many, occasions such as this one, the last days of something endearing — those places that were part of local life seemingly for ages but whose tenures were in fact like the Zephyr at Pontchartrain Beach, racing down its last incline, gone before we knew it, and leaving only a trail of sentiment behind. Those of us on the sidelines might have hoped for one last ride. Instead they zipped past us, blurs from the past: D. H. Holmes, Terry & Juden, Gold Seal Creamery, Godchaux's, Kreeger's, Gus Mayer, Pontchartrain Beach itself, and Schweikhardt's, home of the last of the great drugstore food counters.

Some of the losses are due to various urban and economic maladies, others are no more than the natural progression of things — styles change; people grow old and their kids want a different career; growing competition from the big, slick chain operations — all elements of economic Darwinism.

But when the loved ones gather for the last time, the cause does not matter as much as the fact of the demise. "It's hard to believe you won't be here any longer," one of the regular customers said to Lovie, a jovial counter waitress, who along with Viola was one of Schweikhardt's resident celebrities. There were no doubt many who depended on the store on South Carrollton to get their prescriptions filled, but the place will be best remembered by those who went there to get their appetites satisfied. The writing on the bottom of the menu board assured that all meat, seafood and fowl was cooked fresh on the grill. In its last days, just the heat of business kept the grill smoking. The same was true of the stove on which stood the pot that contained the last batch of Viola's Friday special — her gumbo, which on this, its final day of being served, would allow me to have a brush with immortality.

To accompany the fried fish I had ordered, I had asked for a cup of gumbo. Moments later, the guy on the stool next to me asked for a bowl of the same. Just as I was spooning down the last bit of what was in my cup, the waitress returned from surveying the pot to tell the customer that there was no more. I sat their quietly as it occurred to me that I had probably made gumbo history, having had the last of Viola's.

It was a mild gumbo, not too thick but not too thin, which perfectly complemented the fish. This and a Coke made a complete lunch. That might have been all I had if I had not remembered there was another item for which the place was famous — its nectar soda. There is some debate around town about who was first with the delicacy that is now all but extinct — the classic New Orleans nectar soda. When Katz & Besthoff drugstores had food counters they served the pink sodas, but the folks at Schweikhardt's laid claim to having been first, and I have no reason to dispute that. Unfortunately, they may have been last, too. On this day the sodas were being lined up for customers who knew enough to order them. "Give me a small one," I pleaded. But they only came in one size, a large glass with scoops of vanilla ice cream piled through the sweet froth.

By this time the crowd was getting so big I gave up my spot at the counter. I stood in the back just to feel the ambiance of it all. There was that same sort of criss-crossed emotion that a person might feel at a jazz funeral — sadness because of the departed, joy from the music. A man standing next to me noted the volume of business the place was experiencing that day and somehow captured the irony of such occasions as he said to me, "You know, if everyday was a closing day, the place wouldn't have to close."

But sentiment, like gravity, is a force that only seems to propel things when they are on the descent. The band played as another roller-coaster reached the end of its run, and we could only hope that the next one to come would not be too close behind.

The Departed

A Jazz Wake

To the right of the band was a coffin. The musicians had gathered on this Friday night to pay their respects to Chester Zardis, Sr. Between songs some of those who knew his music spoke, including a producer who had done a documentary about Zardis and who described the musician as the "last of the first jazz bass players."

Outside, cars rushed along the remains of North Claiborne Avenue, the street the I-10 Expressway tried to ruin. Streets, like people, may not be eternal but their history cannot be denied. The black neighborhoods that surround the avenue gave birth to many jazz musicians; the funeral homes that line it prepared them for their final marches.

Zardis' own history was as one of those seminal figures who was there not only when jazz evolved but when those who were part of that evolution were themselves evolving. He was a contemporary of young Louis Armstrong, with the two following similar paths not only in playing music but in facing the music as well — both served time in the detention home for "colored waifs." Both also became jazz innovators on their musical instruments. It is the misfortune of bass players, however, to be out of the spotlight not only on stage but in public perception. Those who know the music know differently, and they know that Zardis was a pioneer in what was called the "slap bass," a method of stroking the strings with a full hand. Butch Thompson was one who knew. Thompson, best known as the pianist from public radio's "Prairie Home Companion," told those gathered that Zardis had been one of his heroes. He remembered how thrilled he had been to play in a band with Zardis, and he recalled how the bass player would grimace when someone's sound wasn't quite right but would glow with an approving glance when the music was working.

Zardis would have likely approved of the performance by these musicians, some of whom had gathered less than three months earlier to celebrate his 90th birthday. The location then was the Palm Court Cafe in the French Quarter, where the old musician had gratefully listened to the music and then whispered a thank you. Now the scene had shifted to the Duplain Rhodes Funeral Home where the whispers were of sorrow. The music, however, was of joy as the group led by trumpeter Percy Humphrey heralded the saint who, we were told, would one day be marching in. Jazz funerals are better known than jazz wakes, but in the confines of a small room the experience becomes more soulful, especially as the musicians begin to wail about "That Old Rugged Cross." Music is supposed to move the spirit as it did during the performance of "By and By" when Percy Humphrey's brother, Willie, rose from among the spectators to begin singing. Mourners as they rocked with the ages have wondered about life, death, suffering and pain. And the spirituals have tried to answer — perhaps evasively but certainly melodically: "We'll understand — by and by."

Meanwhile, in a side room visitors were signing a registry book. There is a certain pride among some musicians, especially on such occasions among colleagues where what they play is as important as their name, and the book was signed accordingly: Frank Mitchell — trumpet; Chris Burke — clarinet, Kerry Brown — drummer. Even rank among Mardi Gras Indians was noted by the signature of "Chief Tootie Montana."

Watching all of this, I wondered how long such pride would continue. The troubling question about New Orleans' traditional jazz is what will happen when the old-timers are gone, when all of the last of the firsts have been carried away. My thoughts were interrupted by a young man who began shaking hands with people as he entered the room. He seemed to be in his early 20s and was dressed casually. As he stopped to shake my hand, I was impressed by what seemed to be his warmth. "By the way," I asked, as he moved on to the next person,

"What's your name?" "James Andrews," he said, and then added with obvious pride, "young trumpet player."

Before leaving, I took a final glance into the room with the coffin. In another room coffee and sandwiches had been served, so now some folks were socializing while others were saying goodbye to Chester Zardis. There were rich folks, poor folks, family folks, friend folks and musical folks. Included in that number was "James Andrews—young trumpet player," meeting more people, shaking more hands.

I walked out to North Claiborne still wondering if the music was dying, yet somehow feeling more confident that it might live on.

THE PARTING

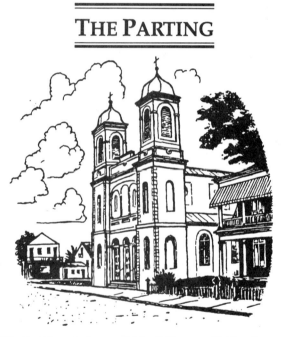

Holy Trinity Church is an old building on St. Ferdinand Street in the Faubourg Marigny neighborhood. It once served the German Catholics who lived in the area; now it serves anyone left. On a Saturday afternoon some people gathered there for memorial services for an acquaintance who had died from what is now all too familiarly described as "complications caused by AIDS." It was a quiet and peaceful ceremony to which the old pipe organ added some harmony. There was little ceremony, just prayers and eulogies. Friends and a priest spoke, although at times the speaking system was too low for much to be heard. But the message was clear: He was human. He could be ornery at times. But he was caring. He was good company. He knew disappointment. He experienced joy. He loved. He was loved. He will be missed. He is gone.

The person being remembered had done some acting in his career, and now he was part of a scene being staged more often than can be comprehended. People hear the statistics, but it is in places such as old churches in old neighborhoods that those numbers become human. The pipe organ's song seems to give testimony that statistics have souls.

After the services, those who had come to remember him went to a reception at his home. A friend had baked a cake. Someone had brought some cookies and chips. There was a pot of coffee and soft drinks. On a table were copies of his vita and his audition photos, the stuff of a performer looking for a greater role. Someone played a tape of "Evita," itself a tribute to a performer who died young.

Those things push the emotions out of whack as though one response triggers the opposite: People who are laughing one moment are hugging and crying in another, then smiling again. Tragedy and comedy, their masks the symbol of theater, are twins, one needed to balance the other. A friend who works for a hospice program told a story about the phenomenal work being done locally so that AIDS patients can be spared the hospital in their final days and at least be able to die peacefully at home. In the process of this caretaking, new relationships are struck. As the story goes, a social worker had been visiting a woman who was dying from the condition. During the social worker's last visit the woman told her, "this may be the last time I see you." "Yes," the social worker responded sadly. "Of course," the dying woman added, "I might see you again on the other side." The social worker nodded. Then the woman smiled and said, "If so, let's do lunch."

It was on a Sunday this past Spring when I had last seen Julian. The occasion was the showing of the AIDS quilt at the Convention Center. Across a floor built large enough to stage a trade show was the quilt, each large patch depicting, according to the design of friends and family, the life of an AIDS patient. A woman we know was there showing her kids the patch made for her brother, their uncle. Across the room a person at the podium read to a somber beat the names of some of those who had died. The list was long; the readings continued.

We were on the way out when we spotted Julian. He was working what seemed to be a rather lonely detail, manning an AIDS information table at the opposite side of the quilt from the podium, but certainly within hearing distance of the drone of its message. In this, one of his final public appearances, he was playing before a small house, but it may have been his most important role. Our conversation was brief though difficult to end, because, in this case, saying goodbye

101

seemed too definite. Where words fail, mumbling sometimes has to suffice, so it was a mumble that closed our last conversation.

Those who knew him better had the chance to be more articulate. They were pleased that he was able to die at home and that the death was peaceful and painless. He had even had time to label all of his possessions so that each was tagged with the name of someone to whom it was bequeathed. One friend got his answering machine. His television was labeled to go to Lazarus House, a local shelter for AIDS patients. Another friend got a print sketch of Cafe du Monde, another a drawing of the performers in the musical, "Company." Pictures, objects, machines, all were tagged so that their lives could continue.

Meanwhile it was the music from "Evita" that provided the harmony, just as the old organ in the church had done an hour earlier. "Don't cry for me," the dying Evita pleaded, though her nation did. And on St. Ferdinand Street there was some comfort that the church doors were closed, there being no further call, for the moment at least, for eulogies of those who died young.

ANNIVERSARIES

MANDINA'S AT SIXTY

In a town known for both rituals and eating, Tommy Mandina remembers an eating ritual. Every other Tuesday when he was a kid, Mandina accompanied his father and mother as they took the Canal Street streetcar downtown to Galatoire's to experience the classic New Orleans dishes.

Now Tommy Mandina himself operates a great New Orleans restaurant, one which is part of other peoples' rituals. Go to Mandina's often enough and among those in the crowd you will see regulars, some positioned at their usual spot at the bar or at their usual table.

Who are those people? In the early days they were most often folks in the oil and gas business. Now the mix is as varied as Mandina's menu, but certain elements of the courthouse crowd are among the most recognizable. One thing about spotting regulars: once you have seen them enough to know they are regulars you have probably become one yourself.

Not that they need an excuse, but at some point this year those regulars at the bar should lift a glass to Mandina's, which is celebrating its sixtieth anniversary. The way Tommy Mandina figures it, the restaurant's numbering system goes back to 1932. There had been a place called Mandina's in that building on that same corner of Canal and North Cortez since the early 1900's. It was founded and operated by Sebastian Mandina, Tommy's grandfather. The original Mandina's was a mixed business, a combination barroom, grocery store, sandwich shop and pool hall. In 1932, Sebastian died and his sons Anthony and Frank took over and made the business into a restaurant. In an era when cities were still growing, Mandina's was a neighborhood restaurant that developed with the neighborhood around it.

Among the best creations to ever come from the city's neighborhoods are its neighborhood restaurants, many of which combined the richness of Sicilian cooking with the abundance of Louisiana seafood. The list of such restaurants is as impressive as is the collection of the city's grand French-Creole restaurants, with Mandina's being the Antoine's, or perhaps the Galatoire's, of its class. Better yet, it may be in a class of its own, since few restaurants of any type offer the same mixture of ambiance, performance from the kitchen and waiters who become like family.

One of my own measures of a restaurant's sense of New Orleans is whether or not its bar serves a Sazerac, the city's grand old sipping drink served in a proper Sazerac glass. Mandina's bar does. Its menu epitomizes local cooking even in the way that the old New Orleans families would match certain meals to certain days. Monday, of course, was red beans and rice day; Sunday, it was roast. Thursday was a red sauce day, either on spaghetti or with a hefty bruccialone. My personal favorite from the Mandina's menu is its corned beef and cabbage, served on Saturday and Tuesday, which may be the world's greatest example of just how flavorful anything can be made to be if the people in the kitchen know what they are doing. Garlic salt, black pepper, crushed red pepper, onions, bacon drippings and knowing how long to let the cabbage cook are part of the dish's success. The other part is the sheer magic of the kitchen. Many of the recipes were handed down from the family; a few are adaptations. The brown sauce that covers the trout meuniere was created by a black chef who was adept at the techniques of soul cooking. The traditional butter-based sauce would burn if it stayed in a pot on the stove too long. A different sauce, one that could be relied on throughout the day, was needed. The soul sauce was the answer. Some dishes are so good they have been sanctified by a family name: The Hilda Salad, one of the city's great and bountiful chef salads, is named after Tommy Mandina's mother.

From 60 years worth of crowded tables there are a lot of stories to tell, including a personal experience.

It happened this past February on the first Saturday of Carnival parades. As was a custom, several of us would gather at Mandina's for lunch in preparation for the Pandora parade, the first each season to march along Canal Street. I had to leave our table briefly to pick up a shirt at a nearby laundry. On the way back, I was walking along Canal just as the lead units of the parade were passing. Since it was raining I used the plastic wrap that protected the shirt to cover my head. A policeman on the communications van at the front of the parade noticed my plight and signaled me to hop on board. Many people have arrived at Mandina's front door through the years, but I may have been the first to have been delivered there by a parade.

That moment seemed like the ultimate New Orleans experience: a parade, Mandina's, even the sprinkled tuxedo shirt that was now hanging from a coat hook in the restaurant. Much has changed over the last 60 years: the Canal Streetcar line is gone; some of the parades may have passed for the last time. There is, however, a certain continuity that comes with the arrival of a perfect oyster poor-boy properly dressed. The rain had intensified, making the afternoon a bit drearier. Yet we are a city that survives life's dampness, perhaps in the spirit of knowing that, no matter what, there's always a warm bread pudding on the way.

THE FAIRMONT AT 100

It was the hotel for the nineties — albeit the 1890's.

One hundred years ago this December, the hotel now known as the Fairmont first opened. During its century, the business had two other names: the Grunewald (December 1893-1923) and the Roosevelt (October 1923-November 1965). But the best known names are those of the people it has housed — the celebrities who are part of the building's lore. When people write about the building, they usually tell tales of Huey Long, who held the Roosevelt so near the center of his universe that when LSU needed a band director, the governor naturally thought to give the job to the leader of the hotel's orchestra. There is Seymor Weiss, the hotel owner during much of its Roosevelt days

who became a Long crony and who handled the candidate's campaign fund. Then there are the entertainers, the stars who performed in the Blue Room, the hotel's fabled nightclub. Their autographs are on several generations of now yellowed napkins and matchbook covers, saved as souvenirs from special nights at the Blue Room.

There is another name that comes to mind: Johnny Fennich. As far as I know, no one ever got Fennich's autograph, unless it was somebody who admired people who were proficient at sitting in hotel lobbies. Fennich spent so much time sitting in the hotel's plush red chairs that many people figured he worked there. He didn't. He just liked the lobby. I was aware of Fennich because I liked the lobby, too. The linear block-long space is one of the last of the grand hotel waiting areas, designed before the days when planners and accountants figured out that fewer chairs might influence more people to patronize the bars instead. To me a hotel's lobby has been a sort of downtown living room — a place to rest and to people-watch. Johnny Fennich, a slight man with gray hair, watched a lot of people during his life, so many that people began watching him watch the people. He and the clock became fixtures.

One time I wondered if he had become even more of a Fairmont fixture than I thought possible. I was in San Francisco in the vicinity of Nob Hill where the Fairmont's sister hotel stands. Being a fan of grand old hotels, I walked in to check out the lobby. It was busy, filled with folks coming and going and people-watching, too. Then I noticed something that stunned me. Sitting in one of the plush chairs was a man of slight build with gray hair who looked just like . . . "No," I thought to myself, "it can't be." I discreetly walked past the chair a couple of times to see if Fennich was doing a split shift. It wasn't him, but it did make me think that every hotel with a grand lobby needs a Johnny Fennich, a spectator to a world in which all the residents live amidst glamour if only until the return flight home.

I once sang with the Coasters in the Blue Room — sort of. The group was performing its collection of oldies and was mid-lyric in the song, "Charley Brown." The lead singer was walking through the audience. Just as he sang the words, "That Charley Brown, he's a clown . . . " he popped the microphone in front of my face, to which I reflectively responded, in a failed imitation of the recorded voice, "Why's everybody always picking on me?" People laughed and clapped but the Coasters stopped short of taking me on the road.

There's another great institution along the hotel's lobby — the Sazerac bar. The bar is my special-occasion place. In fact, the day my ship finally comes in (it's been a slow boat), I will toast its arrival at the Fairmont. I will do so with a Sazerac in hand. The drink is one of the bar's two specialty drinks, for both of which it has owned legal rights. The other is the Ramos Ginn Fizz, an unlikely mixture of milk, gin and orange essence that somehow works. The bar is also know for its murals which show 1930-ish scenes of New Orleans. Generations of drinkers have wondered who those people in the mural are and if one of the characters is supposed to be Huey Long. The people watching continues — even when the people being watched are on the walls.

Hotels are best appreciated as places where out-of-towners stay, but they are appreciated more for the hold they have on locals. Few buildings in the city evoke as much hometown nostalgia. There's a generation of New Orleanians that even remembers the hotel from a distance. In the days of big bands, the music of the Blue Room orchestra was broadcast to the nation each week on WWL radio and, for a while, over the CBS radio network. To many Louisianians on the road, the words "Live From the Roosevelt Hotel" were a link with home. If only they could be among the beautiful people — dancing at the Blue Room.

As the hotel begins its second century, the Fairmont folks have been giving the building a restoration overhaul. (The Blue Room, once gold, is now blue again.) It should be a grand place for the lobby-watchers of the future to behold. Meanwhile, it is tempting to think that those two decades of radio signals from the Blue Room are somehow still racing through the cosmos and that somehow, some way, Johnny Fennich is tuning in.

Invaders

The Tale Of The Rat

We begin with denial. Certainly the gnawing sound that seemed to be coming from behind the stove was being made by a dog that was outside or beneath the house. But that bit of self-assurance began to dissolve as we noticed a trail of pecan shell fragments leading towards a slight opening between the stove and a counter. Then there was an actual sighting, the hind legs and tail disappearing behind a corner. At first we tried to avoid the "R" word, preferring to refer to the intruder as a mouse, but few mice can leap stairs or chomp on purses and cushions like this one could. With more sightings, the ugly truth had to be conceded. There was a rat in the house. A state of war existed.

I would have preferred a humanitarian solution. Once, when a pigeon entered the house, I got rid of it by leaving a trail of cookie crumbs which the bird followed out the door. A wasp will usually find its way out if you open a window wide enough and shoo it in the right direction. But rats don't take hints. They hide and dart about and do sinister things. If only it could have cooperated, maybe it could have undergone corrective rehabilitation or been sent to summer camp or a social worker might have been called in. I wished it would have decided to leave on its own by whatever means it first entered. Instead, the rodent kept on behaving like a rat. It was time to bring on the hardware.

That necessitated a trip to the hardware store, where I thought I found a benevolent contraption that would do damage to neither the rat nor me. It was a device that could be plugged into an outlet. According to the label, it emitted a sound humans could not hear but that to a rodent sounded like the equivalent of a 747 taking off. Unless the rat had had experience as a luggage handler, I reasoned, this might work.

It didn't. The small print on the label went on to explain that the sound waves could only travel in a straight line. Apparently, unless the rodent would have positioned itself in front of the machine, maybe to boogie to the melodies of a 747, it would hear no pain. Back to the hardware store.

I didn't want poison, because worse than having a live rat in the house is having a decaying rat behind some wall. There was the traditional rat trap which seemed too much like cruel and unusual punishment. Another device lured rats inside it, then snapped shut. Its manufacturers took a politically neutral stand by explaining on the label that once the rat was trapped I could deal with it as I chose. Perhaps I could take it dancing.

I settled on a product which consisted of two plastic trays, each filled with sticky stuff. Scattered across the surface of each were little pellets which rats would recognize as a meal. In theory, the perpetrator would go for the pellets and then get stuck on the tray. According to the instructions all I had to do was pick up the tray with a dustpan, place it in a garbage bag and the problem was solved. The offensive had begun.

That evening no more than 20 minutes had passed after the lights were out when I heard a rustling sound. I hurried to the room where the trap was, flicked on the light and there it was. After all these months we finally came face to face. It was fiendish and devious looking. It might have thought the same about me.

I followed the instructions: dust pan, garbage bag. The bag was placed outside, where the rat was left to deal with its future. Maybe it escaped. I never checked to find out.

Inside the house there was a sense of relief followed by a disturbing thought: What if there was another one? To date it seems like there was only a single perpetrator working alone. It might still be on the prowl today if only it had learned a lesson that can be applied to all of us: Whenever you hear a 747 landing in the kitchen, it's best to move on.

ME AND THE RAT: THE SEQUEL

Prologue: *In the last issue, this column told the tale of trying to get rid of a rat in the house while at the same time trying to be sensitive and humanitarian, although the rat was hardly willing to cooperate. After several trips to the hardware store, the trap that was settled on was a plastic tray containing a glue-like gel, hereafter referred to as "sticky stuff," with rat food pellets scattered throughout. The rat in search of a pellet as a snack would get stuck in the sticky stuff. It worked. At the time of the last writing there was no evidence of another rat. The tale continues:*

Only two evenings had passed since I had declared the home to be a rat free zone. I was still feeling victorious, having purged the home of the enemy, when I suddenly fell victim to the household equivalent of sniper fire. My jubilation had been shattered by a sudden sighting of tiny hind legs zooming past a counter. During the next few days there was once again that disturbing gnawing sound coming from behind the walls. The victory celebration was over. The enemy had sent in reinforcements.

I once talked to a man whose job it was to repair streetcars at the Willow Street car barn. He revealed to me one of his discoveries from his career's work. "I'll tell ya' something," he said, "streetcars don't have roaches. Buses," he continued, "they have roaches. But not streetcars." He went on to theorize that the sound of a metal wheel on a steel rail somehow drove roaches crazy — and away. Buses, which ride on rubber, offered no such discomfort to the roaches.

I wish there could be such an inherent quality in my home that would send rats packing. If only the hum of the microwave or the flicking of a TV remote switch had the same impact on rats as metal on metal apparently has on roaches. But no, there was no easy answer. Back to the glue traps.

This rat seemed wiser than his predecessor, skillfully avoiding the sticky stuff. So I decided to increase the bounty. Next to the pellets that were already in place I put a dollop of peanut butter, the crunchy type. Certainly a rodent that gets thrills from gnawing at labels on bottles would consider this to be dinner at Antoine's.

It didn't.

I purchased two more sets of the traps, so that one evening there were five in place. The following morning, one of the traps finally caught something — me. I guess it was inevitable, but I stepped in a tray. I quickly learned just how sticky the sticky stuff was. It was as though a chain reaction had been set off. The rag that I wiped my shoe with became sticky; so did my hands, so did everything I touched in the kitchen, so did my steering wheel when I drove to work. If rats can giggle, this one must have been in hysterics as it peeked from its hideout.

It might have had the last laugh, had it not been for a fluke discovery. One evening while fixing pasta I accidentally threw away the plastic cap that topped a bottle of grated parmesan cheese. So that I wouldn't waste the rest, I enclosed the bottle in one of those zip-snap plastic bags, and left it on the counter overnight. The next morning something had gnawed a hole in the bag in an apparent attempt to get at the cheese. There are those rare moments in life when a solution to a problem suddenly reveals itself in an unexpected manner. The rat had tipped its hand. The peanut butter offensive had failed, but now there was a new bait.

Late one evening, I put a clump of the grated parmesan on one of the trays. I turned off the light. The trap was set.

Only a few minutes had passed before I heard a rattling sound. I hurried to the kitchen, flicked on the light, and faced the invader. Following the instructions that came with the traps, I lifted the tray and its occupant with a dust pan, placed it in a garbage bag and carried the bag outside. The rat, at least, went with a generous serving of parmesan.

It turned out that the rodent had an associate which was soon collared by the same method. Since then, there has been absolutely no sign, or sound, of uninvited guests. There's peace in the house again, and once more some lessons have been learned. One is to always watch where you step; and the other is that when you eat parmesan cheese, be sure it's spaghetti that it is on top of.

ABOUT THE AUTHOR

Errol Laborde has won many journalism awards and is the only three-time winner of the Alex Waller Award, the New Orleans Press Club's highest honor for editorial achievement. He is also a three-time winner of the Press Club's Ashton Phelps Award for editorial writing.

Laborde is Editor/Associate Publisher of *New Orleans Magazine* and Publisher/Editor of *Louisiana Life Magazine*. He also serves as producer and panelist for "Informed Sources," a weekly news discussion program produced by public television station WYES TV, Channel 12.

Laborde holds a Bachelor of Arts degree from McNeese State University and a Master of Arts degree and Ph.D. in Political Science from the University of New Orleans.

ABOUT THE ARTIST

Arthur Nead is from a family of artists. He credits his grandfather, Monte C. Nead, for giving him his early art training. Nead has a Bachelor of Fine Arts degree from Ohio University. He also studied art at the University of London's Goldsmith's College School of Art. Nead is a former staff artist for *Gambit* newspaper. He has illustrated Errol Laborde's "Streetcar" columns originally in *Gambit* and, since June, 1989, in *New Orleans Magazine*. Nead's illustrations were also featured in Laborde's book, "I Never Danced With An Eggplant (On A Streetcar Before)." He is currently a technical writer and editor for Martin Marietta.